SIX FEET UNDER

SIX FEET UNDER

A GRAVEYARD GUIDE TO MINNESOTA

Stew Thornley

Minnesota Historical Society Press

www.mnhs.org/mhspress

The Minnesota Historical Society Press is a member of
the Association of American University Presses.

Manufactured in Canada

10 9 8 7 6 5 4 3 2

∞ The paper used in this publication meets the minimum
requirements of the American National Standard for Information Sciences—Permanence for Printed Library Materials,
ANSI Z39.48-1984.

Title pages: Richard and Jeanne Livingston of Minneapolis
decorated the grave of their uncle, who died in France during
World War I, about 1935

International Standard Book Number 0-87351-514-5

Library of Congress Cataloging-in-Publication Data
Thornley, Stew.
    Six feet under : a graveyard guide to Minnesota /
    Stew Thornley.
        p. cm.
    Includes bibliographical references and index.
    ISBN 0-87351-514-5 (pbk. : alk. paper)
        1. Cemeteries—Minnesota—Guidebooks.
        2. Minnesota—Guidebooks.
        3. Minnesota—Biography.
        4. Minnesota—History, Local.
        I. Title.
F607.T48 2004
977.6′053′092—dc22

2004011427

*To Brenda, my number-one
travel partner in visiting the dead*

SIX FEET UNDER

ACKNOWLEDGMENTS

Deborah Swanson, Alan R. Woolworth, Greg Britton, and Dean Thilgen of the Minnesota Historical Society were particularly helpful with their support and sharing of expertise. Other helpful society staff members include Ruth Bauer Anderson, Tracey Baker, Patrick Coleman, Ellen Miller, Steve Nielsen, Kathryn Otto, Maureen Otwell, Ann Regan, Sally Rubinstein, Terry Scheller, Hampton Smith, John van Vliet, and Marilyn Ziebarth. Will Powers channeled the idea for this book from his very much living wife, Cheryl Miller, to the press.

Dawn Cameron, Jeanette Boothe, and Kim Benson-Johnson are colleagues who had many valuable suggestions on entries for the book. Marc Hugunin, Roger Godin, Paul Maccabee, Sunny Worel, Brad Zellar, George Rekela, Susan Hunter Weir, and Aaron Isaacs were among those who looked over the entries to ensure their accuracy. Steven Hoffbeck provided useful information, as did Larry "Bucky" Bangs.

I was able to visit all the graves located in Minnesota that are listed in this book. Numerous friends accompanied me on these journeys, including my wife, Brenda Himrich, as well as Mark Daly and Brian Augustin of KARE television, who spent two days cruising cemeteries with me in October 2003.

Finally, many thanks to all the city clerks, funeral-home directors and staff members, cemetery workers, and others who assisted me in tracking down graves.

SIX
FEET
UNDER

INTRODUCTION

Burial sites—crypts, graves, niches, ossuaries—engage our minds and emotions.

Similar sentiments were expressed in 1966 by Lewis Younger, president of the Winona County Historical Society, at a ceremony to erect a marker for the graves of the Wisel family, victims of a flood one hundred years before. "History is a never-ending trail of our country," Younger said. "It is important that we save what we have in our communities and preserve it for future generations, as it becomes a living story. By placing markers, it stimulates the imagination of people."[1]

Cemetery surfing has become an increasingly popular hobby in the past decade. People making treks include genealogists tracing their roots, scientists seeking clusters of graves with a common death date that may indicate an epidemic, artists and writers admiring the monuments and epitaphs, travelers looking to get off the beaten path, and people such as myself, who enjoy tracking down the final resting spots of the famous and infamous. Visitors respond in different ways to what they encounter, taking pictures, making rubbings, leaving offerings.

For some, the fascination is the cemetery itself, not the individual graves. In Minnesota, cemeteries may come in different sizes, be found in different settings, cater to different clientele, and vary in age. Some burying grounds are a repository of an area's history.

In certain places, cemeteries are part of a traveler's normal itinerary. Ever since the burial of President John F. Kennedy there, Arlington National Cemetery outside Washington, D.C., has become a major tourist attraction. The Freedom Trail in Boston takes visitors to several cemeteries.

Usually, though, one has to make a cemetery a specific destination, not merely a way point. During the last ten years, I have started making more detours to see graves, both around the country and across Minnesota.

Just getting to the graveyards is part of the fun—cruising into parts of a state or city one would never dream of going to otherwise. As in life, where the journey can be as intriguing and fulfilling as the destination, so it can be with tracking down the dead.

As for the destinations—a cemetery is often an oasis of green space and serenity within a teeming urban area or a haven of humanity down a lonely country road.

Although it may seem strange to think of them in this way, graveyards are inviting places. Many cemeteries welcome visitors, inviting them to come and enjoy their peaceful settings. More than one hundred years ago, recreational excursions to cemeteries were common. City planners, recognizing people's desire for open spaces, began planning these types of sites but without graves, resulting in places such as Central Park in New York City. Cemeteries today are returning to earlier attitudes, with some hosting tours. For example, Woodlawn Cemetery in Winona, Minnesota, holds an annual Cemetery Discovery Walk, during which event visitors are greeted by characters, in costume, telling the stories of their lives while standing beside their graves. Jim Tipton, creator of the Find A Grave website, summed this attitude up with the comment, "I've always loved cemeteries and think of them as parks for introverts. You can go to relax and not have to worry about anyone trying to strike up a conversation; there's no volleyball, either."[2]

Of course, guests must be respectful, both to the grounds and graves and to others who visit cemeteries. Curious bystanders (of which I am normally one) must be careful not to intrude on those who are there to grieve.

In determining the entries for a book on the graves of notable Minnesotans, the first question is, "Who is notable?" Celebrities are always notable, but notable people are not always celebrities. And it has been the non-celebrities who are often the more intriguing to investigate and locate. Every person has a story, of course. A grave bears witness to that story, and its marker can be a physical representation of the person in one way or another.

This book records my personal journey through Minnesota graveyards (and some places farther afield). Another traveler, with a different viewpoint, would choose a different assortment of individuals to investigate, but these are the ones who appealed to me the most during this trip. I have been attracted by individuals whose lives have a connection to my personal interests—such as sports and military history—and also to those whose experiences and talents cover a wide range of life within my home state and its history. Their stories are here arranged in categories to bring together what they have in common and to display some of their dissimilarities. In a few cases, people whom I included had little connection to the state except for their death and interment. Nevertheless, they will be dead in Minnesota much longer than they were alive anywhere else.

While some may find a hobby of visiting graves to be morose or even macabre, I find nothing morbid in seeking out history through cemeteries. There is much to be learned from our past, and one of the liveliest ways to do it is through our dead.

Individuals in this book are referred to by the names by which they are usually known. The popular football star and wrestler is called "Bronko" instead of "Bronislau" Nagurski, for example. A name in italics in an entry indicates an individual for whom there is a separate entry.

PUBLISH AND PERISH

AUTHORS, ARTISTS, AND ARCHITECTS

Whether in literature, theater, fine arts, music, or other forms of artistic expression, Minnesota has much to offer its residents and visitors. Many of the state's creative talents are famous nationally or internationally, and many are home favorites.

DARRAGH ALDRICH (CLARA ALDRICH)
December 31, 1884–March 31, 1967
Lakewood Cemetery, Minneapolis, Hennepin County (Metro Region); section 31, lot 157, grave 7

A teacher, poet, and radio commentator, Aldrich was a pseudonymous writer whose first novel, *Enchanted Hearts,* was made into a Broadway play and later a movie, *A Prince There Was.* She was also a columnist for the *Minneapolis Tribune* and a commentator at WCCO radio in the 1940s. A stately and imposing woman, Aldrich was noted for her sense of humor and for wearing large, magnificent hats, even while broadcasting.

JOHN BERRYMAN
October 25, 1914–January 7, 1972
Resurrection Cemetery, Mendota Heights, Dakota County (Metro Region); section 60, block 34, grave 107

Berryman was a brilliant and troubled poet and a Regents' Professor at the University of Minnesota. He received the Pulitzer Prize in Poetry in 1965 for *77 Dream Songs* and the National Book Award in 1969 for *His Toy, His Dream, His Rest: 308 Dream Songs.* Berryman committed suicide by jumping off the Washington

Avenue bridge over the Mississippi River in Minneapolis in January 1972.

EMMA L. BROCK
June 11, 1886–August 17, 1974
Lakeside Cemetery, Hastings, Dakota County (Metro Region)

Born in Montana, where her father was building Fort Shaw for the U.S. Army, Brock attended the University of Minnesota and then studied at the Minneapolis School of Art and the Art Students League in New York. She wrote and illustrated her first book, *Runaway Sardine,* in 1929 and wrote and illustrated more than thirty books for young readers during her life, many based on her extensive travels.

LEROY S. BUFFINGTON
September 22, 1847–February 16, 1931
Lakewood Cemetery, Minneapolis, Hennepin County (Metro Region); section 2, lot 122, grave 5

LeRoy S. Buffington, about 1895

An architect who received (but later lost) a patent for his revolutionary system in the steel-skeleton method of construction for skyscrapers, Buffington had a role in designing some of the most significant nineteenth-century buildings in Minneapolis, including several that still stand on the University of Minnesota campus—Nicholson Hall (originally built as the chemistry laboratory), Pillsbury Hall, and Eddy Hall. Buffington also designed the second Minnesota state capitol, but his most notable work was the (now-gone) West Hotel, Minneapolis's first grand hotel, which opened on Hennepin Avenue in 1884.

MARY COLTER
April 4, 1869–January 8, 1958
Oakland Cemetery, St. Paul, Ramsey County
(Metro Region); block 66, lot 26

Partially raised and now buried in St. Paul, Mary Colter
was a prominent architect in the southwestern United
States and is well remembered for her role in designing
many of the structures at Grand Canyon National Park,
including the Hopi House, Hermit's Rest, Lookout Studio, and the Watchtower at Desert View. An admirer of
Native American architecture, Colter used Hopi, Zuni,
Navaho, and Mexican motifs in her work.

FRANCES DENSMORE
May 21, 1867–June 5, 1957
Oakwood Cemetery, Red Wing, Goodhue County
(Southern Region); block K, lot 229 (corner of
Densmore & Summit Aves. within cemetery)

The Densmore family home in Red Wing looked out
over the Mississippi River, and often during her childhood Frances would hear Dakota music drifting over
from nearby Prairie Island. As a musician and ethno-
grapher (dealing with the scientific description of specific human cultures), Densmore began recording
Native American music in 1907 and traveled across the
country to record the songs of many different tribal
groups, including some whose cultures were threatened
with disappearance. She recorded nearly twenty-five
thousand songs on wax cylinders, including more than
five hundred Ojibwe songs.

FRANCES CRANMER GREENMAN
June 28, 1890–May 24, 1981
Lakewood Cemetery, Minneapolis, Hennepin County
(Metro Region); section 9, lot 397B, grave 4

A vivacious and nationally known Minneapolis artist,
Greenman was noted for her portraits of celebrities, in-

cluding conductor *Emil Oberhoffer* and actresses Mary
Pickford and Dolores Del Rio. She also was a columnist
for the *Minneapolis Tribune*. Greenman's official governor's portrait of *Karl F. Rolvaag* hangs in the Minnesota
State Capitol.

HARRY WILD JONES
June 9, 1859–September 25, 1935
**Lakewood Cemetery, Minneapolis, Hennepin County
(Metro Region); section 4, lot 264, grave 2.5**

An architect who arrived in Minneapolis in 1883, Jones
designed houses, churches, and commercial buildings
in the city. His work includes the Butler Brothers warehouse (now Butler Square) and the exterior of the
chapel at Lakewood Cemetery as well as a superintendent's building at Loring Park and two restroom buildings at Lake Harriet, which are now the oldest buildings
in the Minneapolis Park System. In late 1911 the Minneapolis Millers baseball team selected Jones for the
renovation of (vanished) Nicollet Park, a massive over-
haul that included a Tudor-style entryway building,
which also housed the team's offices, in the ballpark's
right-field corner.

LES KOUBA
February 3, 1917–September 13, 1998
**Lakewood Cemetery, Minneapolis, Hennepin County
(Metro Region); section 3, lot 499, grave 3**

Kouba was a nationally known wildlife artist and recipient of the first lifetime achievement award from the
Minnesota Waterfowl Association. He was the artist for
the state's first waterfowl stamp and twice designed federal duck stamps. The designer of a number of commercial logos for a variety of companies and products,
Kouba also invented a drawing device called the Art-O-
Graph. His distinctive grave marker features a represen-

tation of an artist's palette and the words "In dedication to his lasting gift to mankind—Portraying with brush and pen—The beauty and majesty of woods, fields and wildlife."

CARVEL LEE
April 2, 1910–August 30, 1998
Lakewood Cemetery, Minneapolis, Hennepin County (Metro Region); section 36, lot 457, grave 5

Lee was an author and illustrator of more than one hundred books. She began her career working in advertising as a commercial artist. Her first books were textbooks, but she wrote on a variety of topics with one of her best-selling books being a local travel guide, *36 One-Day Discovery Tours: Fun Places to Drive within and from Minneapolis and St. Paul.*

SINCLAIR LEWIS
February 7, 1885–January 10, 1951
Greenwood Cemetery, Sauk Centre, Stearns County (North Central/West Region); Lewis family plot, 3 rows in & 8 monuments to left of main entrance

A Pulitzer Prize-winning novelist (who turned down the award) for the novel *Arrowsmith,* Lewis is best remembered for his 1920 best-seller, *Main Street,* a not-so-complimentary story about small-town life that caused controversy in his hometown. Although some residents were outraged at his portrayal of the fictional town of Gopher Prairie, believed to be modeled after Sauk Centre, the city later embraced the author and now touts its main thoroughfare as the Original Main Street. In 1930 Lewis became the first U.S. writer to receive the Nobel Prize in Literature "for his vigorous and graphic art of description and his ability to create, with wit and humour, new types of characters."

MAUD HART LOVELACE
April 25, 1892–March 11, 1980
**Glenwood Cemetery, Mankato, Blue Earth County
(Southern Region); lot 55, block 2, section D, space 1**

A native of Mankato, Lovelace wrote poetry and short stories before embarking on historical novels, including *Early Candlelight,* which was set at Fort Snelling. In 1940 she began writing the beloved Betsy-Tacy books, a series of tales and adventures based on her childhood. The stories take place in the fictional town of Deep Valley, although

Maud Hart Lovelace, 1931

the setting was Mankato in the early-twentieth century. Lovelace wrote ten books in the series during the next fifteen years and is well remembered in her hometown. A wing of the Minnesota Valley Regional Library in Mankato is named for her, and in 1979 the Mankato Friends of the Library established the Maud Hart Lovelace Book Award for children's books.

EMMANUEL MASQUERAY
September 10, 1860–May 26, 1917
**Calvary Cemetery, St. Paul, Ramsey County
(Metro Region); section 40, block 43, lot 9**

The designer of the soaring St. Paul Cathedral and St. Mary's Basilica in Minneapolis, Masqueray arrived in the Twin Cities in response to a request by Archbishop *John Ireland.* The two had met in St. Louis, where the French-born Masqueray had been the chief of design for the 1904 World's Fair. His handsome likeness appears in relief on his grave marker, which was erected "by his friends" in his adopted home.

GEORGE MORRISON

September 30, 1919–April 17, 2000

Chippewa Cemetery, site of former Chippewa City settlement, near Grand Marais, Cook County (Northeast Region)

An internationally known artist, Morrison was born and is now buried in Chippewa City, a long-gone settlement near the Grand Portage Indian Reservation along the north shore of Lake Superior. He studied in Minneapolis, New York City, and Paris. His works are in the Minnesota Museum of Modern Art in St. Paul, the Minneapolis Institute of Arts, the Tweed Museum of Art in Duluth, the Whitney Museum of American Art in New York, and the Art Institute of Chicago. A member of the Grand Portage Band, Morrison also helped create and develop the American Indian Studies Department at the University of Minnesota in the 1970s. He was equally skilled in creating haunting images of the Superior horizon in paintings and also assemblages of found wooden pieces, some being fragments found on the lake's shore.

George Morrison in his studio, 1993

OLE E. RØLVAAG

April 22, 1876–November 5, 1931

Oaklawn Cemetery, Northfield, Rice County (Southern Region); section K, lot 85, grave 5

Author of novels, poems, and textbooks, Rølvaag was professor of Norwegian language and literature at St. Olaf College in Northfield. His internationally acclaimed novels, including *Giants in the Earth* and *Peder Victorious,* were originally published in Norwegian and later issued in English. Rølvaag was knighted by King

Haakon VII of Norway in 1926. He was the father of
Karl F. Rolvaag, who used an Americanized spelling
of the family surname and served as governor of Minnesota from 1963 to 1967.

BATISTE SAM
October 3, 1914–January 25, 1998
**Vineland Cemetery, Vineland, Mille Lacs County
(North Central/West Region)**

A storyteller and elder in the Mille Lacs Band of Ojibwe,
Sam was a nationally known crafts worker who conducted tours and performed craft demonstrations for
more than thirty years at the Mille Lacs Indian Museum
near Onamia. In 1997, a few months before her death,
Sam was named Tribal Elder of the Year by the National
Congress of American Indians for her contributions in
preserving traditional Ojibwe art, history, culture, and
language.

THE FINAL ADVENTURE

SOME HEROES AND
OTHER BRAVE SOULS

Minnesota can claim many brave and adventurous people, some of whom became known around the world for courage and some who were heroic in everyday life.

JOHN BEARGREASE
1855–May 29, 1915
Chippewa Cemetery, Beaver Bay, Lake County (Northeast Region)

The namesake of Minnesota's annual sled-dog race along the north shore of Lake Superior, John Beargrease was a member of the Grand Portage Band of Ojibwe. A hunter, trapper, fisherman, and sailor, he is best remembered for carrying the U.S. mail between Two Harbors and Grand Marais, and sometimes all the way up to Grand Portage, in the late-nineteenth century. Depending on the season and the conditions, he made the trek by boat, on foot (often in snowshoes), or by sled and is credited with a role in the development of the North Shore, as his legendary mail runs provided residents with a link to the outside world. Beargrease is interred on a hillside in Beaver Bay under a monument listing the names of all buried on the site.

JOHN W. BLAIR
April 27, 1853–January 29, 1922
Oakland Cemetery, St. Paul, Ramsey County (Metro Region); block 46, lot 107

An African American, Blair was the porter in charge of the chair car on Limited Train Number 4 of the St. Paul and Duluth Railroad Company on September 1, 1894, the day that Hinckley and much of the surrounding area was destroyed by a fire that killed more than four hundred residents. Heading south from Duluth, Number 4 stopped when the engineer saw the flames and reversed direction after picking up many fleeing citizens. With some of the cars on the train burning, Blair wet towels and gave them to the passengers to wrap around their heads while also calming the passengers, particularly the children. He also pulled down a fire extinguisher and sprayed passengers whose clothes or hair had started on fire.

TOM BURNETT
May 29, 1963–September 11, 2001
Fort Snelling National Cemetery, Minneapolis, Hennepin County (Metro Region); section 7, grave 23

A Bloomington native, Burnett was one of the passengers reported to have taken part in a revolt against the terrorists who had hijacked United Airlines Flight 93 on September 11, 2001. Three other planes commandeered by terrorists had already been intentionally flown into buildings, in New York City and outside Washington,

D.C. Passengers on Flight 93, aware of the fate of the other planes, apparently organized an attack against their hijackers, and it is believed that this is what caused the plane to crash in an empty field in Pennsylvania, killing all aboard. Burnett's grave marker includes the inscription "Citizen Soldier / Flight 93."

Tom Burnett's grave marker, 2003

CONSTANCE CURRIE
March 18, 1890–November 14, 1957
**St. Mary's Cemetery, Minneapolis, Hennepin County
(Metro Region); section 7, block 9, lot 3, grave 1**

A pioneering and dedicated social worker, Currie was
director of Neighborhood House in St. Paul for nearly
forty years and served as the United States delegate
to the International Conference of Settlement Houses
in 1931.

GLEASON GLOVER
June 14, 1934–August 24, 1994
**Fort Snelling National Cemetery, Minneapolis,
Hennepin County (Metro Region); section B, grave 305–6**

An African American native of Virginia who grew up
during segregation, Glover arrived in Minneapolis in
1967, at a time when the city was experiencing racial
strife, and became the first full-time executive director
of the Minneapolis Urban League. Although confrontation was then a prevalent response to such tensions,
Glover chose a different style, one geared more toward
coalition building. This approach angered some civil
rights supporters although Glover, with his conciliatory
yet firm methods, remained in the job for twenty-five
years and oversaw significant progress. His achievements
included a court challenge that opened the city's fire
department and other institutions to minority groups
and the organization of boycotts against local products
and businesses over discriminatory practices in hiring
and treatment of customers, which resulted in changes
in diversity policies in the targeted companies. Upon
Gleason's death, Matthew Little, the former head of the
Minneapolis chapter of the National Association for
the Advancement of Colored People, called him a
"giant in the area of civil and human rights."

OWEN HAUGLAND
August 20, 1891–July 29, 1929
City Cemetery, Springfield, Brown County (Southern Region)

Haugland was an endurance flyer who was fatally injured when his plane crashed at Wold-Chamberlain Field (now Minneapolis-St. Paul International Airport) in July 1929. During the burial in Springfield, Thorwald "Thunder" Johnson, Haugland's friend and former copilot, circled the cemetery in his airplane and dropped a wreath of roses and then a shower of flowers on the grave.

JOSEPH HEYWOOD & NICOLAUS GUSTAFSON
Joseph Heywood, August 12, 1837–September 7, 1876
Nicolaus Gustafson, August 20, 1846–September 11, 1876
Northfield Cemetery, Northfield, Rice County (Southern Region)

Heywood and Gustafson died during and after a raid on the First National Bank in Northfield on September 7, 1876, by Cole Younger, two of Younger's brothers, and five others, probably including Jesse and Frank James. Gustafson, a Swedish immigrant who did not speak English and did not understand the bandits' command to leave, was fatally shot outside the bank. Heywood, the bank's acting cashier, was shot and killed after bravely refusing to cooperate with the robbers and open the (empty) vault. Two members of the gang were killed by citizens in the street while the robbery took place. One other was killed and three others (including the Youngers, who were later sentenced to the Minnesota State Prison at Stillwater) were captured two weeks later by a posse. Two members of the gang, believed to be the James brothers, escaped and never were captured.

CHARLES "SPEED" HOLMAN
December 27, 1898–May 17, 1931
**Acacia Park Cemetery, Mendota Heights, Dakota County
(Metro Region); Cedar section, block 13, lot 10, grave 1**

Less than two years after the death of fellow aviator
Owen Haugland, Holman died in similar fashion. Raised
in Minnesota, Holman actually earned his nickname
while racing motorcycles. He later became interested in
flying and flew air-mail routes for Northwest Airlines.
Holman's greatest racing achievement came in 1930,
when he won the Thompson Trophy Race. He was
killed when his racing airplane crashed in Omaha,
Nebraska, the following year. The airport in St. Paul—
Holman Field—is named for him. Holman is buried
on the highest point in Acacia Park Cemetery.

Charles "Speed" Holman, about 1930

OLLI KINKKONEN
1881–September 18, 1918
**Park Hill Cemetery, Duluth, St. Louis County
(Northeast Region); section G, row 29, lot 15**

Near the graves of the *Duluth lynching victims* in Park
Hill Cemetery is that of Olli Kinkkonen, a Finnish immigrant reportedly lynched in 1918 for refusing to join
the military. He had been kidnapped and tarred and
feathered by a vigilante group that pressured men to
fight in World War I. A few weeks later, Kinkkonen's
body was found hanging from a tree outside of Duluth.
His death certificate gives "suicide by hanging" as the
cause of death, with some sources claiming that, humil-
iated by the tar and feathering, he had hanged himself.
The inscription on the grave marker for Kinkkonen
proclaims that he was a "Victim of warmongers."

MAO VANG LEE
November 3, 1933–September 24, 2003
**Forest Lawn Memorial Park, Maplewood, Ramsey County
(Metro Region); block 32-D, lot 149A, grave 3**

A Hmong American, Mao Vang Lee was born in a small
village in northeastern Laos near the Vietnamese border. Her obituary states that she was a "well-respected
woman who assisted and advised the Lee family, the
families of soldiers, and other helpless people who
suffered" during the Vietnam War. She arrived in the
United States in 1978.

LOUISE RIORDAN
November 19, 1886–August 7, 1916
**St. Mary's Cemetery, Minneapolis, Hennepin County
(Metro Region); section 28, block 1, lot 9, grave 26 (unmarked)**

A waitress who began unionizing female workers in
1911, Riordan served as secretary-treasurer of the Trades
and Labor Assembly of Minneapolis and was a stalwart

member of the advisory board of the Minimum Wage Commission of Minnesota.

RON RYAN, TIM JONES, & LASER
Ron Ryan, June 26, 1967–August 26, 1994
**Union Cemetery, Maplewood, Ramsey County
(Metro Region); block 31, lot 734**

Tim Jones, October 31, 1957–August 26, 1994
Laser, died August 26, 1994
**Elmhurst Cemetery, St. Paul, Ramsey County
(Metro Region); block 50 south, lot 262.**

On the morning of August 26, 1994, Ryan, a rookie St. Paul police officer, responded to a seemingly innocent call about a man sleeping in a car in a church parking lot on the city's East Side. When Ryan arrived, the man fatally shot him. Tracking the suspect later that morning, another officer and his police dog, Tim Jones and Laser, were both shot to death by the same man. These were the first killings of St. Paul cops in twenty-four years. After spectacular and moving public funerals, Ryan was buried in Maplewood, while Jones, along with Laser's ashes, was buried in St. Paul.

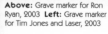

Above: Grave marker for Ron Ryan, 2003 **Left:** Grave marker for Tim Jones and Laser, 2003

SCHOOL'S OUT

TEACHERS AND EDUCATORS

One of the reasons Minnesota is often rated high on lists of the best places to live is the quality of education in the state. This is reflected in the lives of teachers and educators buried in Minnesota, from those who have started and taught in small but significant schools to the famed builders of the University of Minnesota.

IRVAMAE APPLEGATE
September 18, 1920–March 5, 1973
**Oak Knoll Cemetery, Princeton, Mille Lacs County
(North Central/West Region); east side of Arborvitae
Lane at south end of cemetery**

Applegate was the dean of the School of Education at St. Cloud State College (now St. Cloud State University) from 1962 to 1973. During that time, she served as president of the Minnesota Educational Association and later the National Education Association.

HARRIET BISHOP
*January 1, 1817–
August 8, 1883*
**Oakland Cemetery, St. Paul,
Ramsey County (Metro
Region); block 10, lot 29**

Bishop established the first public school, as well as the first Sunday school, in St. Paul. The schoolhouse was at Third and St. Peter Streets. A native of Vermont and a

Portrait of Harriet Bishop, painted about 1880

graduate of Catharine Beecher's pioneering teacher-training course for women in New York, Bishop responded to a call for a teacher from Presbyterian missionary Thomas Williamson and arrived in St. Paul, landing at Kaposia, in July 1847. She was also a writer of poetry and history.

ANNE BOARDMAN
July 20, 1899-March 7, 1986
Lakewood Cemetery, Minneapolis, Hennepin County
(Metro Region); section 21, lot 347, grave 6

Boardman was a teacher and chairman of the English Department at the University of Minnesota. She also wrote articles and short stories and was the author of the books *Such Love Is Seldom* and *Good Shepherd's Fold.*

LOTUS D. COFFMAN
January 7, 1875–September 22, 1938
Sunset Memorial Park, Minneapolis, Hennepin County
(Metro Region); Community Mausoleum, Chapel level,
corridor 4, section 14, tier B

Coffman, whose mother had called him Lotus Delta after a character in a novel, was recruited in 1915 from the University of Illinois to strengthen the School of Education at the University of Minnesota. A very practical man despite his dreamy name, Coffman succeeded in that mission and then served as president of the university from 1920 to 1938, overseeing a campus construction boom as many of the buildings on the mall were built, before dying in office. During his tenure, Coffman was a strong supporter of the General College.

SOLOMON COMSTOCK
May 9, 1842–June 3, 1933
**Prairie Home Cemetery, Moorhead, Clay County
(North Central/West Region); lot 98**

A community leader in Moorhead and a state legislator, Comstock helped establish what is now Minnesota State University at Moorhead. A colleague of *James J. Hill,* Comstock helped build a railroad system in the Red River Valley. His daughter, Ada, was the first dean of women at the University of Minnesota and later became president of Radcliffe College.

BORGHILD DAHL
February 5, 1890–February 20, 1984
**Lakewood Cemetery, Minneapolis, Hennepin County
(Metro Region); section 7, lot 238, grave 6**

The Norwegian American Dahl overcame blindness and prejudice against the disabled to become a high-school principal in Minnesota for more than ten years and a professor at Augustana College in Sioux Falls, South Dakota, from 1926 to 1939. She wrote many books for young readers, including novels and the autobiographical *I Wanted to See,* and received the St. Olaf Medal from King Haakon VII of Norway in 1950.

CHARLOTTE DAY
December 24, 1917–May 3, 1989
**Nett Lake Cemetery, Nett Lake, Bois Forte Indian Reservation,
St. Louis County (Northeast Region)**

Born in Ontario, Day grew up on the Bois Forte Indian Reservation, south of International Falls. She moved to St. Paul in 1967 and was instrumental in forming the Red School House, a sister school to the Heart of the Earth Survival School in Minneapolis, magnet schools for Indian children. Day, the mother of seventeen, pulled her children out of the St. Paul public school system and enrolled them in the Red School House, where she was active in many ways, including as a cook, counselor, and member of the board of directors.

MARY JACKSON ELLIS
March 21, 1916–March 3, 1975
Lakewood Cemetery, Minneapolis, Hennepin County (Metro Region); section 60, lot 652, grave 2

Ellis was the first full-time black teacher in Minneapolis and nationally recognized as an innovator in teaching children. Ellis also wrote children's books and teaching-aid publications.

WILLIAM WATTS FOLWELL
February 14, 1833–September 18, 1929
Lakewood Cemetery, Minneapolis, Hennepin County (Metro Region); section 5, lot 165, grave 2

A major in the Union army during the Civil War, Folwell was only thirty-six years old when he became the first president of the University of Minnesota in 1869. During his fourteen-year tenure, the university campus doubled in size, a medical department was organized, and an experimental farm was purchased. Folwell was later a professor of political science at Minnesota. In his old age, he often received valentines sent to him from Minnesota schoolchildren on his birthday, Valentine's Day.

RICHARD GREEN
May 27, 1936–May 10, 1989
Crystal Lake Cemetery, Minneapolis, Hennepin County (Metro Region); section 24, lot 211, space 12

Green served as the superintendent of public schools in Minneapolis from 1980 to

Richard Green, 1982

1988, leaving to take the position of schools chancellor in New York City, where he promoted programs to reduce dropping out, drug use, violence, and substandard buildings. Little more than a year into his tenure in New York, however, Green died of an asthma attack. His determined character is reflected in the inscription on his grave marker, "If it is to be / It is up to me."

Fred King's grave marker, 2003

FRED KING
December 8, 1916–
May 25, 2002
Oakwood Cemetery, Rochester, Olmsted County (Southern Region); section 3, east one-half of lot 194

King was a longtime educator and prolific writer of school books for children who oversaw the Rochester school district's instructional program for seventeen years and rewrote the basic courses of study for a variety of subjects and grade levels.

CANDACE "DACIE" MOSES
January 26, 1883–January 3, 1981
Oaklawn Cemetery, Northfield, Rice County (Southern Region); section K, lot 36, grave 2

An employee and later a part-time librarian at Carleton College in Northfield who lived a block from campus, Moses opened her house for students to play cribbage, rehearse music, cook food, and socialize. Sunday mornings saw the greatest congregation as Carleton students gathered to bake muffins. Moses left her house to the college with the provision that students be allowed to congregate and bake there.

ANDREW ROBERTSON
December 6, 1790–May 11, 1859
**Lower Sioux Agency, Redwood County,
near Morton (Southern Region)**

Robertson was an interpreter and superintendent at the Lower Sioux Agency who served as an interpreter at treaty negotiations in Washington, D.C., in 1858.

DENIS WADLEY
April 21, 1940–May 4, 1994
**Resurrection Cemetery, Mendota Heights, Dakota County
(Metro Region); section 12A, block 7, lot 25, grave 2**

Wadley was an English teacher at De La Salle High School in Minneapolis, as well as a political commentator and activist. After Wadley was diagnosed with terminal cancer in 1992, he eschewed treatment and spoke extensively about society's attitudes toward death.

THAT'S SHOW BIZ

ENTERTAINERS AND MEDIA PERSONALITIES

A few of Minnesota's media stars—Cedric Adams, Dave Moore, Halsey Hall—have taken on legendary status, but many others have made contributions to newspapers, television, and radio. At least one star tiptoed into the state later in life and now is a permanent resident (*see* pages 36–37).

CEDRIC ADAMS
May 27, 1902–February 18, 1961
Lakewood Cemetery, Minneapolis, Hennepin County (Metro Region); section 26, lot 203, grave 5

Adams was a popular author and journalist who had numerous radio and television shows as well as a variety of columns in the *Minneapolis Star.* To help keep up with his prodigious schedule, Adams had a broadcast studio in his Hopkins home as, at his peak, he did more than fifty radio shows and eight television shows a week, occasionally mixing in

Cedric Adams, about 1948

a variety show somewhere in Minnesota, all the while maintaining his newspaper column and humor writing. It has been reported that Adams needed seven secretaries to keep up with the vast amount of fan mail he received, and that airplane pilots flying over his broadcast area could tell when his evening show had ended, as lights below them all went out just after Adams had signed off.

ANNA ANDAHAZY
December 28, 1917–December 1, 1983
**Resurrection Cemetery, Mendota Heights, Dakota County
(Metro Region); section 61, block 40, lot 3, grave 4**

Andahazy was a member of the Ballet Russe de Monte
Carlo before moving in 1946 to the Twin Cities, where
she opened the Andahazy Choreographic School in
St. Paul with her husband, Lorand. She was also the
cofounder and principle dancer in the Andahazy Ballet
Borealis Company of Minnesota from 1952 to 1970.

AXEL (CLELLAN CARD)
June 24, 1903–April 13, 1966
**Resurrection Cemetery, Mendota Heights, Dakota County
(Metro Region); section 6, block 29, lot 2, grave 1**

Best remembered for his popular children's television
show in the 1950s and 1960s, Card had a career in
broadcasting that went back more than two decades
before he assumed the role of Axel. He worked at a
variety of radio stations, starting with WCCO, in the
1930s while maintaining other jobs to provide for his
family during the Great Depression. Card also took part
in the Twin Cities' first telecast, an experimental broadcast by Dr. George Young, who owned WDGY radio,
where Card worked at the time. He later returned to
WCCO and often added a Scandinavian dialect to his
resonant voice, an accent he kept when assuming the
television character of Axel in 1954. Operating without
a script on "Axel and His Dog," which was set in a tree
house, Card also made personal appearances around
the state as kids clamored for Axel. The show continued, although no longer with Axel, after Card died in
1966. His sidekick of several years, Carmen the Nurse
(portrayed by Mary Davies), carried on the program.

IRENE BEDARD
March 10, 1901–January 24, 1959
**Hibbing Park Cemetery, Hibbing, St. Louis County
(Northeast Region); block 1, lot 189, grave 5**

A writer and later the business manager/secretary-
treasurer for the *Hibbing Daily Tribune*, Bedard was
nationally recognized for her stories on foreign coun-
tries. She received the President Cortines Trophy in
1956 for articles on Mexico.

CALLUM DE VILLIER
January 19, 1907–June 12, 1973
**Lakewood Cemetery, Minneapolis, Hennepin County
(Metro Region); section 11, lot 1072, grave 2**

A marathon dancer, de Villier made the Guinness Book
of World Records by dancing 1,448 hours in the Ken-
wood Armory in Minneapolis in 1928 and topped that
total a few years later in Massachusetts when he and a
partner danced for five months, taking only brief medical and restroom breaks during the final three weeks of
their endurance feat.

Callum de Villier's grave marker, 1999

GEORGE ENGESSER & VATES ENGESSER

George Engesser, October 27, 1889–May 14, 1962
Vates Engesser, May 3, 1896–September 13, 1984
Greenhill Cemetery, St. Peter, Nicollet County (Southern Region)

George Engesser got his start in show business when an itinerant vaudeville show arrived in St. Peter in 1909 and was in need of a temporary piano player. George took the job and from there went into vaudeville. He developed his own act and later performed with his wife, Vates. In 1925 the Engessers started their first circus, which became the second-largest motorized one in the United States within a few years. George and Vates's final resting place is adorned by an elephant sculpture.

DICK ENROTH

December 16, 1918–March 23, 1999
Lakewood Cemetery, Minneapolis, Hennepin County (Metro Region); section 27, lot 692, grave 1

A Twin Cities sportscaster, most notably for the Minneapolis Lakers, Enroth was known for his precision (describing the distance of a basketball shot down to the quarter-foot) and rapid-fire delivery. A story is told that Lakers guard Slater Martin, bringing the ball across the mid-court line, paused near the announcers' table and yelled at Enroth, "Slow down! We can't keep up with you."

WILL FORSHAY

1965–April 8, 2003
Lakewood Cemetery, Minneapolis, Hennepin County (Metro Region); section 34, row 3B, grave 6

A professional skydiver and BASE jumper (a participant in the sport of jumping from stationary objects, such as cliffs, antennae, and high bridges, with a parachute), Forshay was also a member of the Flying Elvi, a ten-member parachute team that jumped while dressed in

Elvis Presley costumes. Overcoming leukemia, Forshay obtained his pilot's license but died in a plane crash while taking copilot training on a jet for an Ohio freight company when the plane crashed short of the Toledo airport.

HALSEY HALL
May 23, 1898–December 30, 1977
Fort Snelling National Cemetery, Minneapolis, Hennepin County (Metro Region); section L, grave 4058

Like *Clellan Card as Axel* and *Marty O'Neill* as the voice of All-Star Wrestling, Halsey Hall is remembered in a specific role by baby boomers—in Hall's case, as the color man for broadcasts of the Minnesota Twins during their first decade in Minnesota—and for his signature exclamation "Holy cow!" But also like the others, Hall had a distinguished career that preceded his notoriety of the 1960s. He carried on simultaneous careers as a sportswriter and broadcaster while mixing in officiating of local sports (including National Football League games when Minneapolis had a pair of teams in the 1920s) and serving as one of the area's most popular toastmasters at banquets and other events. A consummate character and raconteur, Hall was one of the most colorful and beloved media personalities in the Twin Cities.

Halsey Hall interviewed the Minneapolis Millers during a pregame ceremony at Nicollet Park in Minneapolis, September 1955

HARLAN P. HALL
August 27, 1838–April 9, 1907
**Oakland Cemetery, St. Paul, Ramsey County
(Metro Region); block 27, lot 2**

A native of Ravenna, Ohio, Harlan Page Hall arrived in
Minnesota in 1862 on the recommendation of another
Ravenna native, *Henry Swift,* who was serving in the
Minnesota Senate at the time and became governor of
the state the following year. Several other family members followed Harlan to Minnesota, including his older
brother, Halsey R. W. Hall, who became the grandfather
of future sportswriter/broadcaster *Halsey Hall.* The Hall
family was involved in newspaper work, and Harlan,
after working briefly as a compositor for the *St. Paul
Press,* along with a partner purchased the *St. Paul Pioneer* (which later became the *St. Paul Pioneer Press*) for
twenty-five thousand dollars. Although he and his partner retained ownership of the *Pioneer* for less than a
year, Harlan stayed in the newspaper game and made it
his career. He founded the *St. Paul Dispatch* in 1868 as
part of his effort to further the cause of the Democratic
party. He later founded another Democratic paper, the
St. Paul Globe, after having sold the *Dispatch* to a stock
company, which shifted the newspaper's politics to
support the Republican party.

JOE HENNESSY
June 22, 1912–April 1, 2002
**Fort Snelling National Cemetery, Minneapolis,
Hennepin County (Metro Region); section 16, grave 54**

Hennessy was an award-winning outdoors writer for a
variety of Twin Cities newspapers, including the *St.
Paul Pioneer Press,* where he was also sports editor, and
the *Minneapolis Star.*

CASEY JONES & ROUNDHOUSE RODNEY
(ROGER AWSUMB & D. LYNN DWYER)

Roger Awsumb (Casey Jones), July 10, 1928–July 15, 2002

Acacia Park Cemetery, Mendota Heights, Dakota County (Metro Region); Beech section, block 12, lot 4, grave 15

D. Lynn Dwyer (Roundhouse Rodney),
November 22, 1927–September 3, 1976

Cremated

The television duo of Awsumb as Casey Jones and Dwyer as Roundhouse Rodney entertained children for many years with a variety of shows, most notably "Lunch with Casey," that ran on WMIN-TV and WTCN-TV from 1954 to 1973. Dwyer continued with his own show until he died of a heart attack in 1976. Awsumb resurrected the role of railroad engineer Casey Jones on other Twin Cities television stations, as well as through personal appearances, in the ensuing years. In 1984 Awsumb moved to the Brainerd Lakes region and worked full-time as a broadcaster at KLKS radio until 1993 and continued part-time until his

Right: Roundhouse Rodney and fans, 1960–69 **Below:** Casey Jones (in engineer's attire) and Santa Claus arrived by helicopter at North High School in Minneapolis and met Junior Royalty of the Minneapolis Aquatennial summer celebration, 1955–56

death. Awsumb was named Outstanding Broadcast Personality by the Minnesota Broadcasters Association in 1995 and was a charter member of the Museum of Broadcasting Hall of Fame in 2001.

MARY KYLE
October 27, 1908–July 23, 1994
Fort Snelling National Cemetery, Minneapolis, Hennepin County (Metro Region); section W, grave 1255

Kyle was a managing editor and columnist for the *Twin Cities Observer* and later the *Twin Cities Courier,* a pair of African American newspapers. A free-lance writer and radio and television commentator, Kyle became the first female president of the Minnesota Press Club and the first female board member of the Minneapolis Young Men's Christian Association. She also served on the boards of directors for the Minneapolis Urban League, Phyllis Wheatley Settlement House, and Northwestern National Bank.

CECIL NEWMAN
July 25, 1903–February 7, 1976
Lakewood Cemetery, Minneapolis, Hennepin County (Metro Region); Mausoleum, room 218, tier 4, crypt D

Newman founded the *Minneapolis Spokesman* and *St. Paul Recorder,* the chief sources of black-community news in the Twin Cities, in the 1930s and served as the newspapers' editor and publisher until his death. Active in many civil-rights groups, Newman helped integrate the war industries in the Twin Cities during World War II. *Hubert H. Humphrey* said Newman "helped sensitize me to civil-rights issues" and "was the first editor to support me when I ran for mayor [of Minneapolis in the 1940s]."

BILLY NOONAN
February 18, 1881–February 13, 1957
**Elm Park Cemetery, Baudette, Lake of the Woods County
(North Central/West Region)**

Known as "the Sage of Baudette," Noonan was the editor of the *Baudette Region* for nearly a half century. His editorial barbs were reprinted in newspapers and magazines throughout the state and beyond.

EMIL OBERHOFFER
August 10, 1867–May 22, 1933
**Lakewood Cemetery, Minneapolis, Hennepin County
(Metro Region); section 44, lot 39, grave 3**

A violinist and composer, Oberhoffer arrived in Minneapolis in 1897 and sought to establish a permanent symphony orchestra in the city. He conducted the first Minneapolis Symphony Orchestra in 1903 and continued in that role for nineteen years.

MAYNARD SPEECE
February 2, 1913–September 27, 2001
**Meadowlands Cemetery, Meadowlands,
St. Louis County (Northeast Region)**

Speece was the farm director at WCCO radio in Minneapolis, where he worked from 1952 until 1978, when he suffered a stroke. Speece was one of the best-known personalities on Twin Cities radio as he gave the farm reports amid corny jokes and lively banter with other WCCO personalities.

TINY TIM (HERBERT KHAURY)
April 12, 1932–November 30, 1996
**Lakewood Cemetery, Minneapolis, Hennepin County
(Metro Region); Mausoleum, room 117, tier 2, crypt F**

Born in New York City, Herbert Khaury had little success as a musician until he adopted the falsetto singing voice that became his signature. He performed under a variety of names, finally settling upon Tiny Tim. His personal idiosyncrasies became part of his offbeat act, which featured a ukulele and his one hit song, *Tip Toe Thru the Tulips With Me.* He became a familiar figure on stages and variety shows through the 1960s, and his career peaked with his wedding in 1969 to Victoria Budinger ("Miss Vicki") on *The Tonight Show Starring Johnny Carson,* creating one of the most-watched events in television history. Tiny Tim married Susan Gardner ("Miss Sue"), a Minnesota woman, in 1995 and lived in Minneapolis during his final days. He had just finished performing his trademark song at a Woman's Club of Minneapolis event when he collapsed, later dying in a hospital. Apparently the last thing that Tiny Tim heard was applause.

SELMA TOY
September 30, 1895–August 19, 1986
Lakewood Cemetery, Minneapolis, Hennepin County
(Metro Region); section 36, lot 478, grave 6 (unmarked)

Toy was a speech and drama instructor at the MacPhail Center for the Arts in Minneapolis. She had performed with a troupe of musicians and actors on the Chautauqua circuit in the 1920s and 1930s and was one of the country's few female monologists, performing a soliloquy during which she assumed the roles of all the characters, male and female, in a play and characterized them by voice changes.

"WHOOPEE JOHN" WILFAHRT
May 11, 1893–June 15, 1961
New Ulm Catholic Cemetery, New Ulm, Brown County
(Southern Region); section K, lot 32

Wilfahrt was a rambunctious German American bandleader from New Ulm, best remembered for his vigorous polkas and schottisches. His band played for more than twenty years at Deutsches Haus in St. Paul and for nine years at the Marigold Ballroom in Minneapolis. The "Whoopee" moniker reportedly came when the band was late for an engagement one night, prompting a customer, upon Wilfahrt's arrival, to shout, "Whoopee! John's here!"

"Whoopee John" Wilfahrt, 1937

I TOLD YOU I WAS SICK

MEDICAL PRACTITIONERS

While Mayo may be the first name (or names) in Minnesota medicine, the state has produced many other pioneers in this field, as well as innovative businesses serving the medical industry.

ARTHUR ANCKER
March 20, 1851–May 15, 1923

Old Frontenac Cemetery, Frontenac, Goodhue County (Southern Region); south end of cemetery road

Arthur Ancker, 1898

For nearly forty years, Ancker was the superintendent of City and County Hospital, in St. Paul, renamed Ancker Hospital following his death and later called Regions Hospital. Ancker died after being stricken by faintness while visiting patients at the hospital. News accounts reported that Ancker as a youth in Baltimore administered to his very first patient, a dog with a broken leg. Ancker successfully set the leg with splints that he devised, which may have prompted him to make a career in medicine. Another report said that Ancker set fire to the bedclothes of a patient claiming to be paralyzed as a result of a railroad accident, causing the man to leap from the bed and thus expose the attempted fraud.

ALBERT CHESLEY
September 12, 1877–October 17, 1955
**Fort Snelling National Cemetery, Minneapolis,
Hennepin County (Metro Region); section G, grave 2546**

Chesley was the secretary/executive officer of the Minnesota Department of Health from 1921 until his death in 1955. He served as a medical aide in the Philippines during the Spanish-American War, then joined the state health department and attended medical school. Chesley supervised relief work in Europe during World War I and then served in Poland with the American Red Cross for two years. With the state health department, Chesley developed a code that forbade acceptance of payments by public-health officers for endorsing products. He also persuaded the U.S. Congress to transfer American Indian health and medical care from the Bureau of Indian Affairs to the U.S. Public Health Service. Chesley posthumously received the Sedgwick Memorial Medal, the country's highest public-health honor.

C. WALTON LILLEHEI
October 23, 1918–July 5, 1999
**Fort Snelling National Cemetery, Minneapolis,
Hennepin County (Metro Region); section 6-B, grave 182**

A pioneer, Lillehei performed the first successful open-heart surgery while a professor at the University of Minnesota in the early 1950s. A few years later, Lillehei devised a solution for a group of babies at University of Minnesota Hospital who each had an opening that would not close in their septum, a wall that separates the ventricles of the heart. Lillehei sewed a patch over the opening of the septum, but, in a few of the babies, the sutures in the patch interfered with the electrical conduction of the heart. With the help of other doctors at the hospital, Lillehei developed a pacemaker especially for the babies, one that sent a relatively gentle voltage through wires attached directly to the heart.

LAURA LINTON
April 8, 1853–April 1, 1915

Greenfield Cemetery (also known as Cook's Valley Cemetery), Kellogg, Wabasha County (Southern Region); Old Addition, block 3, lot 10 (tallest monument in northwest quadrant of cemetery)

Linton was a scientist and doctor for whom the substance lintonite is named. In 1879 Linton performed the analysis that established the substance as a mineral, thus earning the honor of having it named after her. Before receiving her medical degree in 1900, Linton was a teacher at Central High School in Minneapolis. After graduation from medical school, she was a physician at Rochester State Hospital.

CHARLES MAYO & WILLIAM MAYO
Charles Mayo, July 19, 1865–May 26, 1939
William Mayo, June 29, 1861–July 28, 1939

Oakwood Cemetery, Rochester, Olmsted County (Southern Region); section 3, Charles: lot 166, William: lot 167

Sons of a country doctor from England who settled in the Minnesota River valley in 1855 and moved to Rochester eight years later, Drs. Charlie and Will, like their father William Worrall Mayo, became pioneers in surgery and developed the internationally known medical establishment that bears their name. When a tornado struck Rochester in 1883, the senior Mayo, along with William, who had just obtained his medical degree, and Charles, who was still in his teens, converted the family home into an improvised hospital to treat the injured. The response to the disaster became the inspiration for a large hospital in Rochester, a vision carried out by the Mayo sons. This hospital, St. Mary's, became the nucleus for the Mayo Clinic, which was formally organized in 1912, and eventually a foundation for medical education and research.

ORIANNA MCDANIEL
October 2, 1872–March 12, 1975
**Lakewood Cemetery, Minneapolis, Hennepin County
(Metro Region); section 24, lot 90, grave 8**

After being graduating from the University of Michigan medical school, McDaniel arrived in Minnesota in 1894 and joined the staff of Northwestern Hospital, one of the few hospitals that accepted female interns at the time. She became the first woman physician at the Minnesota state health department in 1896 and worked for the department for the next half-century, serving as the head of the Division of Preventable Diseases from 1921 until her retirement in 1946 at the age of seventy-four.

KATHERINE NYE & LILLIAN NYE
Katherine Nye, February 27, 1887–March 2, 1967
Lillian Nye, April 22, 1885–July 28, 1972
**Zumbrota Cemetery, Zumbrota, Goodhue County (Southern
Region); section C, lot 147, Katherine: grave 4, Lillian: grave 5**

The Nye sisters were both physicians in St. Paul. Katherine specialized in the health of young women while Lillian worked for the St. Paul public schools and also was a pediatric instructor for the University of Minnesota Medical School for more than fifty years.

WHO SAID OLD SOLDIERS NEVER DIE?

MILITARY FIGURES

In their state's best military tradition, the members of the First Minnesota Volunteer Infantry Regiment distinguished themselves on July 2, 1863, the second day of the Battle of Gettysburg during the Civil War, making a heroic countercharge to stop two Confederate brigades and allow time for General Winfield Scott Hancock's Second Corps to repair the lines in the Union center. "Do you see those colors?" Hancock is reported to have asked William Colvill, commander of the First Minnesota, while pointing to an Alabama flag in the center of an advancing division. "Then take them!"

Charles Powell Adams, sporting the trefoil badge of the Union army's Second Corps, which also appears on his grave marker, about 1862

CHARLES POWELL ADAMS
March 3, 1831–
November 2, 1893
Lakeside Cemetery, Hastings, Dakota County (Metro Region); block 19, lot 6

Adams, a lieutenant colonel in the First Minnesota Volunteer Infantry Regiment, was wounded during the Battle of Gettysburg. He later commanded Hatch's Independent Battalion of Minnesota Cavalry and was discharged with the battalion, at which time he was brevetted brigadier general "for meritorious service."

JAMES ALLEN
May 6, 1843–August 13, 1913
**Oakland Cemetery, St. Paul, Ramsey County
(Metro Region); block 46, lot 34C**

Allen received the Medal of Honor for his actions as a
private in Company F of the Sixteenth New York Infantry during the Civil War. His citation reads, "Single-
handed and slightly wounded he accosted a squad of
14 Confederate soldiers bearing the colors of the 16th
Georgia Infantry (C.S.A.). By an imaginary ruse he
secured their surrender and kept them at bay when
the regimental commander discovered him and rode
away for assistance."

ROLLA BANKS
About 1820 (sometimes given as 1817)–1903
**Woodlawn Cemetery, Winona, Winona County
(Southern Region); section Q, lot 193**

Banks served in Company B of the Third U.S. Volunteer
Infantry during the Mexican War and was a captain in
Company D of the Seventh Minnesota Volunteer In-
fantry Regiment during the Civil War. A native of
Virginia, Banks arrived in Minnesota in 1854 and was
one of the earliest settlers in Winona County.

ORION BARTHOLOMEW
September 4, 1837–September 17, 1919
**Lakewood Cemetery, Minneapolis, Hennepin County
(Metro Region); section 24, lot 167, grave 1**

Bartholomew served in the military from the time of
the news of the firing on Fort Sumter, marking the beginning of the Civil War, until May 1866, when, upon
being mustered out, he was brevetted brigadier general
"for meritorious services during the whole period of the
war." A white native of Indiana, Bartholomew was a
part of a regiment commanded by Benjamin Harrison

before being ordered to organize regiments of African American soldiers. He eventually became colonel of the One Hundred and Ninth Colored Infantry Regiment and was sent to Louisville, Kentucky, to organize several other regiments. For many years, Bartholomew spent summers at a home on Lake Minnetonka; he lived in Minnesota year round by the time of his death as one of six surviving officers of his Colored Infantry unit.

FRANCIS BLISS
August 19, 1793–April 3, 1882
Oakwood Cemetery, Belle Plaine, Scott County (Metro Region); original cemetery, lot 23

A Massachusetts native, Bliss enlisted in the military at the age of twenty in March 1814. Four months later, he was part of the invasion of Canada, fighting against the British in the War of 1812. Bliss was wounded in the leg as his company held off British light infantry in the woods near Chippawa, Ontario. He arrived in Minnesota Territory in the 1850s and later filed a land patent in Scott County, where he farmed near Belle Plaine for the rest of his life.

SAMUEL BLOOMER
November 30, 1835–October 4, 1917
Fairview Cemetery, Stillwater, Washington County (Metro Region); block 4, lot 15

A Stillwater resident born in Switzerland, Bloomer served in the First Minnesota Volunteer Infantry Regiment during the Civil War. Although wounded in the first battle of Manassas (Bull Run), he took part in General George McClellan's Peninsular Campaign in 1862. That September at Antietam, he was shot in his right leg, resulting in its amputation three days later. Bloomer returned to Minnesota that December and spent his remaining years in Stillwater.

ALFRED BRACKETT
May 22, 1826–September 22, 1892
**Roselawn Cemetery, Roseville, Ramsey County
(Metro Region); division 1, lot 365**

Alfred Brackett was the leader of Brackett's Battalion of
Minnesota Cavalry during the Civil War. While in the
south, Brackett engaged *Millie Bronson* as his cook; she
traveled with him during his return to Minnesota,
where she joined the household of Brackett's distant
cousin, *George Brackett.*

HARRY BURAU
December 3, 1899–June 14, 2003
**Knollwood Memorial Gardens, Fergus Falls, Otter Tail County
(North Central/West Region); Garden of Christus, lot 120, D-4**

When he died in June 2003, Burau was reported to be
Minnesota's last surviving U.S. Army veteran of World
War I. He enlisted in September 1918 and was in state-
side training when the armistice came that November
11. Burau then returned to his hometown of Fergus
Falls, where he farmed and was involved in civic activi-
ties, spending thirty-six years on the board of Dane
Prairie Township.

JOSEPH BURGER
April 16, 1848–January 2, 1921
**Oakland Cemetery, St. Paul, Ramsey County
(Metro Region); block 102, lot 10**

Starting his military service as a drummer boy, after
reportedly running away from home and joining the
U.S. Army when he was thirteen and receiving his captain's commission at the age of sixteen, Burger was
attached to Company H of the Second Minnesota Volunteer Infantry Regiment when he was one of a detach-
ment of sixteen men who defended a wagon train at
Nolansville, Tennessee, in February 1863. For his part in

repulsing the attack of 125 Confederate cavalrymen and saving the train, Burger was awarded the Medal of Honor. He was a grandfather of United States Supreme Court Justice *Warren Burger.*

STEPHEN CHANDLER
November 20, 1841–February 1, 1919
Lakewood Cemetery, Minneapolis, Hennepin County
(Metro Region); section 6, lot 100, grave 3

Chandler received the Medal of Honor for action at Amelia Springs, Virginia, on April 5, 1865. His citation reads, "Under severe fire of the enemy and of the troops in retreat, went between the lines to the assistance of a wounded and helpless comrade, and rescued him from death or capture."

WILLIAM CHRISTIE
December 18, 1830–September 19, 1901
Saratoga Cemetery, Saratoga, Winona County (Southern Region)

With his brother Thomas, Christie served in the First Minnesota Battery from 1861 to 1865. He participated in the battles of Pittsburg Landing (Shiloh) and Corinth as well as the siege of Vicksburg. Christie also served with General William Tecumseh Sherman during the Atlanta campaign and during Sherman's destructive march to the sea. Christie was captured by Confederates after the Battle of Bentonville (North Carolina) in March 1865.

WILLIAM COLVILL
April 15, 1830–June 13, 1905
Cannon Falls Cemetery, Cannon Falls, Goodhue County (Southern Region); beneath statue depicting Colvill in his Civil War uniform

Colvill was the commander of the First Minnesota Volunteer Infantry Regiment at the Battle of Gettysburg (*see* page 43) and was among the wounded as his regiment suffered a casualty rate of more than 80 percent during its counterattack on the second day of the battle that turned the course of the Civil War.

PAUL DILLE
April 3, 1893–July 19, 1918
Dassel Community Cemetery, Dassel, Meeker County (Southern Region); block 3, section 6, lot 291, grave 1

Dille was graduated from college on May 24, 1917, and enlisted in the U.S. Marine Corps on the same day. Serving in the Fifty-first Company, Fifth Regiment, he saw six months of service on land and another six on the cruiser *Georgia*. Dille was killed in action at Soissons, France, on July 19, 1918. After nearly three years, his remains were returned to his hometown of Dassel and buried in the community cemetery there in April 1922.

ALFRED GALES
1825 or 1826 or 1838 or 1842–August 3, 1892
Elmhurst Cemetery, St. Paul, Ramsey County (Metro Region); Soldiers' Rest, block 26, lot 14, grave 1

Gales was an escaped slave who helped guide a Third Minnesota Volunteer Infantry Regiment company as it made its way through Arkansas during the Civil War. Gales then enlisted in the regiment and served as a cook in Company B. After being mustered out of the army in 1865, Gales traveled with the Third Minnesota as its members returned home. He took the name of Albert Miller, and lived and worked in St. Paul until his death. He is buried under his slave name.

CHARLES E. GODDARD
May 14, 1846–December 9, 1868
Woodlawn Cemetery, Winona, Winona County (Southern Region); section H, lot 42

Lying about his age, Goddard enlisted in the Union army during the Civil War when he was fifteen (but said that he was eighteen) and served in Company K of the First Minnesota Volunteer Infantry Regiment. He participated in some of the deadliest actions of the war, including the First Minnesota's suicide charge at Gettysburg. His health weakened by military service, "Charley" died at the early age of twenty-three back home in Winona.

LYMAN KIDDER

August 31, 1842–early July 1867

Oakland Cemetery, St. Paul, Ramsey County (Metro Region); block 28, lot 2

A veteran of the Civil War who had also fought in the Dakota War of 1862 in Minnesota, Kidder was a second lieutenant in Company M of the Second U.S. Cavalry in the summer of 1867 when he and a small patrol left Fort Sedgwick in Colorado with a dispatch for Lieutenant Colonel George Custer, who was protecting railroad construction from Indians. On July 12, in northwestern Kansas, Custer found the remains of Kidder and his men, who had apparently been killed by Cheyenne and Sioux approximately ten days earlier. The remains were buried in a mass grave at the site. The grave was opened the following March, and Kidder's father identified his son by a distinctive shirt collar, then took his remains to St. Paul for reinterment.

CHRISTIAN MARGUTH & ELISE MARGUTH

Christian Marguth, June 19, 1881–January 7, 1934
Elise Marguth, May 2, 1890–January 14, 1976

Birch Coulee Battlefield State Historic Site, Renville County (also in Redwood County) (Southern Region)

A native of Switzerland, Christian Marguth was a horse-shoer with Troop K of the Fifteenth U.S. Cavalry during World War I. He arrived in Minnesota in 1926 and opened a blacksmith shop in Morton. Marguth became the first person buried in an area that was to be platted for a veterans' cemetery as part of the Birch Coulee Battle Field Memorial State Park (now Birch Coulee Battlefield State Historic Site) outside Morton, the site of a battle during the Dakota War of 1862. An impressive ceremony was held in 1934 for Marguth's interment, but only one more burial was ever made at the site, that of his widow, Elise, in 1976.

JOHN S. MARSH
About 1834–August 18, 1862
Fort Ridgely Cemetery, Fort Ridgely State Park and Historic Site, Nicollet County (Southern Region)

A Union veteran of the first battle of Manassas (Bull Run) in the Civil War in July 1861, Captain Marsh was the commander of Fort Ridgely when the Dakota War broke out in Minnesota thirteen months later. With forty-six enlisted men and an interpreter, Marsh was on his way to the Lower Sioux Agency when his troops encountered Dakota at Redwood Ferry. At least a dozen soldiers were killed and Marsh, attempting to escape by leading his troops downstream, drowned while trying to cross to the south side of the Minnesota River. He and other members of his unit are buried in a mass grave at Fort Ridgely Cemetery.

JOHN MCCONNELL
June 14, 1846–May 27, 1943
Oakwood Cemetery, Belle Plaine, Scott County (Metro Region); original cemetery, lot 106

McConnell joined the Union army in 1863 and was a private in Company C of Brackett's Battalion of Minnesota Cavalry. When he joined the battalion at Fort Snelling in early 1864, it was preparing for the Northwestern Indian Expedition. McConnell was the last known surviving veteran of the 1864 expedition and, as his grave marker proclaims, "The last man" of Brackett's Battalion.

MARTIN LUTHER NICKS

Died March 14, 1864, aged 26

**Minneapolis Pioneers and Soldiers Memorial Cemetery
(Layman's Cemetery), Hennepin County (Metro Region);
block M, lot 63, 8th grave from the southwest**

Nicks had been in an unmarked grave at Layman's Cemetery when a new Grand Army of the Republic section was established for Union veterans of the Civil War. He was one of the first soldiers to be transferred to the new section. Unbeknownst to those involved in the re-interment, Nicks, who was born in Hampshire, Tennessee, had been a Confederate soldier.

SAMUEL PHILLIPS

January 29, 1845–November 12, 1915

**Oakland Cemetery, St. Paul, Ramsey County
(Metro Region); block 46, lot 57**

A private in Company H of the Second U.S. Cavalry, Phillips received the Medal of Honor for "gallantry in action" during the Indian campaigns at Muddy Creek, Montana, in May 1877.

FRANCIS SAMPSON

February 29, 1912–January 28, 1996

**St. Catherine's Cemetery, Luverne, Rock County
(Southern Region); section B, block 119, lot 2**

"Father Sam," a Catholic chaplain for the U.S. One Hundred and First Airborne Division, parachuted into Normandy on D-Day, June 6, 1944, and later had some of his adventures depicted in two World War II movies, *The Longest Day* and *Saving Private Ryan*. Many paratroopers landed in three or four feet of water. Sampson sank into water over his head but managed to cut himself free from his parachute. Then he dove down several times to retrieve his equipment for saying Mass. (This scene was enacted in *The Longest Day*.) Sampson was later ordered to find Fritz Niland (the real Private Ryan), a paratrooper whose three brothers had been during killed the week of the invasion, and remove him from combat as soon as possible. Sampson escorted Niland to Utah Beach; from there he was sent to London and finally back home to the United States as his family's sole remaining son.

Francis Sampson's grave marker, 2003

JOHN B. SANBORN

December 5, 1826–May 16, 1904

Oakland Cemetery, St. Paul, Ramsey County (Metro Region); block 2, lot 71–74

The adjutant general of Minnesota in 1861, Sanborn organized the state troops for the Union at the beginning of the Civil War. He was brevetted major general in 1865. Sanborn served in both the Minnesota Senate and House of Representatives.

MARSHALL SHERMAN
1822–April 19, 1896

Oakland Cemetery, St. Paul, Ramsey County (Metro Region); block 41, Soldiers' Rest

Sherman was a private in Company C of the First Minnesota Volunteer Infantry Regiment that countered Pickett's Charge at Gettysburg on July 3, 1863. Sherman captured the battle flag of the Twenty-eighth Virginia Infantry Regiment during the battle and received the Medal of Honor for his actions. The flag is now in the collections of the Minnesota Historical Society.

Marshall Sherman and captured flag, about 1864

JAMES MILLARD TAWNEY
March 18, 1887– November 22, 1918

Woodlawn Cemetery, Winona, Winona County (Southern Region); section H, lot 75

Tawney was a member of Company C of the Second Minnesota National Guards, assigned to the Mexican border in 1916. He resigned to take a position with an exporting/importing house in Japan. When the United States entered the war against Germany in April 1917, Tawney left Japan for Winona, only to find that his vacancy in Company C had been filled, so he went to Washington, D.C., and was commissioned a first lieutenant in the Signal Reserve Corps. Promoted to captain, Tawney was put in charge of the Student Army Training Corps in Valparaiso, Indiana. He did not make it to the European battlefront. Instead, Tawney became ill with pneumonia and died in Valparaiso just eleven days after the armistice. Tawney's father, *James A. Tawney,* served in the U.S. House of Representatives.

STEPHEN TAYLOR
March 23, 1757–June 2, 1857
Woodlawn Cemetery, Winona, Winona County (Southern Region); lot 45, section P

A Revolutionary War veteran, Taylor was first buried in an unmarked grave in a prairie cemetery south of Winona and then in Woodlawn Cemetery in town until a headstone, proclaiming him "one of the heroes of Ticonderoga," was dedicated in 1880. It has since been established that Taylor did not fight with Ethan Allen at Fort Ticonderoga in 1775 (especially since his birth year of 1757 is also doubtful), but not before a replica of the fort was erected around the headstone, making his the most distinctive grave in the cemetery. Taylor was part of the First Massachusetts Regiment of the Continental Army under George Washington. He continued to live in the East after the war until arriving in Minnesota Territory with about a dozen family members in 1854. A year later he qualified for bounty

Stephen Taylor's grave marker, 1933

land under an act of Congress pertaining to soldiers. Taylor received 160 acres in Winona County and lived on them until his death.

HUDSON WHEATON
February 16, 1840–April 8, 1896
**Evergreen Cemetery, Caledonia, Houston County
(Southern Region); block D, lot 65, grave 5**

Born in Chautauqua County, New York, Wheaton settled in Houston County in 1859. During the Civil War, he was a member of the Second Minnesota Battery, Light Artillery.

JOHN LOGAN WILLIS
June 23, 1794–January 30, 1872
**Caledonia Cemetery, Caledonia, Houston County
(Southern Region)**

Willis was a veteran of the War of 1812. A resident of Wayne County, Kentucky, he enlisted in November 1814, served in Colonel Slaughter's regiment of the Kentucky Detached Militia, and took part in the Battle of New Orleans in 1815. After the death of his wife, Frances, in 1869, Willis moved to Caledonia, Minnesota, and from then on lived with one of his children, who had moved there in 1856.

ALBERT WOOLSON
February 11, 1847–August 2, 1956
**Park Hill Cemetery, Duluth, St. Louis County
(Northeast Region); section S, row 4, space 13**

Woolson was the last surviving member of the Union army from the Civil War. Son of a man who lost a leg during the April 1862 battle at Shiloh, Woolson joined Company C of the First Minnesota Heavy Artillery in October 1864. His first assignment was as a drummer.

PACHAO XIONG
May 29, 1935–October 19, 2001
**Oakland Cemetery, St. Paul, Ramsey County
(Metro Region); block 26, lot 6A**

Xiong was a member of the Lao National Army who
was recruited by the U.S. Central Intelligence Agency
in 1963. Xiong was a combat soldier and served with
the CIA until the end of the Vietnam War in 1975.
He was a member of the Lao Veterans Organization
until his death.

Pachao Xiong's grave marker, with inscriptions in both English and Laotian, 2004

OTHER REALMS

A LEGENDARY MAN
AND VARIOUS ANIMALS
AND THEIR FRIENDS

An objective of this compilation was to include a variety of individuals in terms of notability. Also striving for diversity among species allowed the inclusion of notable non-human Minnesotans—and even a legend.

A LEGENDARY MAN

PAUL BUNYAN
1794–1899
**Paul Bunyan Memorial Park, Kelliher, Beltrami County
(North Central/West Region)**

Sometimes a man is so legendary that he merits a symbolic grave. There is at least one such grave in Minnesota. This giant lumberjack is a part of Minnesota lore, with a statue of Paul and his blue ox, Babe, being a landmark on Lake Bemidji. A seated statue of Paul Bunyan greeted visitors to Paul Bunyan Land in Brainerd until the amusement park closed in 2003. Even before Paul's demise in Brainerd, the legendary man had a grave, in Paul Bunyan Memorial Park in Kelliher, where a huge burial mound includes his grave marker, complete with birth and death dates that show him to have lived for 105 years.

VARIOUS ANIMALS AND THEIR FRIENDS

DAN PATCH & MARION SAVAGE

Dan Patch, summer 1896–July 11, 1916

**Former site of Taj Mahal stables, Savage, Scott County
(Metro Region); unmarked grave**

Marion Savage, March 26, 1859–July 12, 1916

**Lakewood Cemetery, Minneapolis, Hennepin County
(Metro Region); section 23, lot 92, grave 5**

Dan Patch was the greatest and best-known champion
pacing horse in the world during the early-twentieth
century. The main attraction at state fairs from 1902 to
1909, Dan set a record at the 1906 Minnesota State Fair
of a mile in one minute and fifty-five seconds. Businessman Marion Savage, who owned Dan and the Taj Mahal
stables in what is now Savage and who died about
thirty hours after hearing of his horse's demise, had
wanted Dan stuffed, but Savage's wife, Marietta, instead
had him buried on the grounds of Taj Mahal. The stables no longer exist, but it is believed that Dan Patch
and several other horses are still buried on the site.

Marion Savage drove Dan Patch (left; hitched to racing wagon) and Dazzle Patch (hitched
to sulky), about 1905

DON
1968–January 10, 1994
Science Museum of Minnesota, St. Paul,
Ramsey County (Metro Region)

A coprophilic gorilla at Como Zoo, Don was born in
Cameroon in Africa. At the age of one year, he was
brought to the zoo in St. Paul, where he was a popular
attraction until he died of kidney failure. He was then
stuffed and put on display at the museum.

DON
1857–December 18, 1886
Roselawn Cemetery, Roseville, Ramsey County
(Metro Region); near back entrance

During the Civil War, Don was the horse ridden by
William R. Marshall, commander of the Seventh Minnesota Volunteer Infantry Regiment and later governor
of Minnesota. Don was buried beneath a tree in Roseville in land that became part of Roselawn Cemetery.

DULUTH BEAR
Died August 18, 1929
Grandma's Saloon & Grill, Canal Park, Duluth,
St. Louis County (Northeast Region)

In the summer of 1929 a 350-pound black bear walked
through a plate-glass window into the coffee shop of
the Hotel Duluth. A barrage of chairs thrown by night
watchman Albert Nelson failed to stop him. Equally
futile were attempts to capture the bear alive, so it was
left to Sergeant Eli LeBeau of the Duluth Police Department to bring him down with a rifle shot. The bear was
stuffed and on display at the hotel (later Greysolon
Plaza) for years and is now at Grandma's Saloon & Grill.

KUMA
1952–April 23, 1979
**Science Museum of Minnesota, St. Paul,
Ramsey County (Metro Region)**

Kuma the polar bear was killed at Como Zoo in St. Paul by vandals who hurled large chunks of concrete at her and her companion, Mato. The killers were charged with aggravated criminal damage and sentenced to community service at the zoo, while Kuma was stuffed and exhibited at the science museum.

LOBO
Died 1938
**Morell's Chippewa Trading Post, Bemidji,
Beltrami County (North Central/West Region)**

Lobo was a wolf that killed more than one hundred deer a year while hunting in an area between Red Lake and Lake Itasca in northern Minnesota. Notorious for not feeding on the deer he killed and only drinking the blood of his prey, Lobo evaded trappers, most notably Algot Wicken, for a dozen years. Tangled up in one of Wicken's snares but escaping after breaking the cable, Lobo never again walked into a snare. Two years later Wicken caught Lobo in a trap, one of two he had set on either side of a snare. Lobo was later stuffed and displayed at Morell's trading post.

MR. MAGOO
Died 1968
Lake Superior Zoo, Duluth, St. Louis County (Northeast Region)

A mongoose brought into the United States on a freighter in 1962, Mr. Magoo ended up in the municipal zoo in Duluth but was ordered by the federal government to be deported or destroyed because of a ban on mongooses. The local efforts to keep Mr. Magoo became national news, and eventually Interior secretary

Stewart Udall granted him nonpolitical asylum. Mr. Magoo, who became the subject of children's books, lived at the zoo until his death in 1968 and was then stuffed and exhibited.

WHISKEY
1911–43
Historic Fort Snelling, Minneapolis, Hennepin County, (Metro Region)

Too spirited for the cavalry, Whiskey instead became a polo horse and a performer, serving as the U.S. Army's horse of goodwill. His remains were moved twice because of transportation projects that impeded on his burial sites. On June 14, 2002, he was re-interred on the edge of a bluff overlooking the Mississippi River at Historic Fort Snelling.

HARRIET WOLFGANG & CATS
November 4, 1908–
June 11, 1990
Sunset Memorial Park, Minneapolis, Hennepin County (Metro Region); block 8, section 531, grave 1

Harriet Wolfgang autographed her new book at the Cat's Meow shop in Minneapolis, 1963

Wolfgang was a cat lover as well as a championship breeder and show judge. Her interest in cats began on a Valentine's Day when her husband, Robert, gave her a Siamese kitten. At one time Wolfgang owned more than twenty cats, raising several to All-American status, in her St. Louis Park home, and she traveled around the country to cat shows. She also authored several books on different kinds of cats.

EARLY DAYS

NATIVE AMERICAN LEADERS, PIONEERS, SETTLERS, AND MORE

The Dakota (Sioux) and the Ojibwe (Chippewa) have long been the primary groups of native peoples in Minnesota. This chapter includes the stories of both historical and contemporary Native American leaders in addition to individuals of mixed-blood heritage who had both Native American and European ancestry.

Also included are non-Indian pioneers and settlers, some of whom are now remembered primarily for their interaction with Native Americans during the tragic Dakota War of 1862 (sometimes called the Sioux Uprising), the most significant conflict within its boundaries since Minnesota became a state in 1858. Unhappy with the United States government's failure to meet its obligations under the Traverse des Sioux and Mendota treaties of 1851, a few Dakota men attacked white settlers near Acton in August 1862. The war spread across south-central Minnesota, with Little Crow as the main Dakota leader, and hundreds died until the Dakota were defeated in the Battle of Wood Lake on September 23 by Minnesota militia units lead by Colonel Henry H. Sibley.

ACTON SETTLERS
Died August 17, 1862
**Ness Memorial Cemetery, Litchfield,
Meeker County (Southern Region)**

In Ness Memorial Cemetery outside of Litchfield is a mass grave for five settlers—Robinson Jones, Viranus Webster, Howard Baker, Ann Baker [Jones], and Clara D. Wilson—killed by Dakota on August 17, 1862, in the incident that precipitated the Dakota War.

JEROME BIG EAGLE (WAMINDEETONKA OR WAMDITANKA)
1827–January 5, 1906
**Doncaster Cemetery, near Granite Falls,
Yellow Medicine County (Southern Region)**

Big Eagle was a Dakota chief who joined the Mdewakanton band and later took part in the Dakota War, leading his band in the second battles of New Ulm and Fort Ridgely and in the fighting at Birch Coulee and Wood Lake. He surrendered in September, was tried by a military commission, and sentenced to death, although he was spared the fate of many others, including thirty-eight Dakota who

Jerome Big Eagle, about 1863

were hanged at Mankato by the federal government for war crimes on December 26, 1862, in the largest mass execution in United States history. Big Eagle was given a reprieve and eventually pardoned by President Abraham Lincoln two years later.

ANTOINE JOSEPH CAMPBELL
November 25, 1825–January 9, 1913
**St. Joseph's Cemetery, Montevideo, Chippewa
County (Southern Region); section 3, lot 5, plot 2**

The son of mixed-blood parents, Campbell began trading with Indians at the age of fifteen. With his family, he moved to Traverse des Sioux in 1851 and four years later to the Redwood Agency. With *Joseph LaFramboise,* he was a government interpreter in treaty negotiations of the U.S. government with the Dakota. During the Dakota War, the Campbells were held captive, and

Antoine Joseph was forced to drive *Little Crow* to battles in a carriage as well as act as his secretary for his correspondence with *Henry H. Sibley*. The Campbell family was freed at Camp Release in late September 1862.

CHARLES CHRISTMAS
November 29, 1796–June 17, 1884

Minneapolis Pioneers and Soldiers Memorial Cemetery (Layman's Cemetery), Hennepin County (Metro Region);
block A, lot 37, grave south, 1/23 from north

The first county surveyor in Hennepin County, Christmas made the first survey west of the Mississippi River in Minnesota, in 1851, enabling settlers to establish claim lines in what is now Minneapolis. In addition to being the county surveyor for many years, Christmas was the principal engineer on territorial roads running in and out of Minneapolis and St. Anthony (the area on the east side of the river that is now southeast Minneapolis). Christmas Lake near Excelsior is named after him.

HELIC CLEMENTSON
February 23, 1858–January 19, 1942

Clementson Community Cemetery, Clementson,
Lake of the Woods County (North Central/West Region)

Clementson came from North Dakota to Lake of the Woods County (which was still part of Beltrami County at the time) by way of Warroad and across Lake of the Woods in 1894. He picked out a homestead in the eastern part of the county, across the Rainy River from Ontario, and thirteen years later platted the townsite that took his name. He operated a sawmill in Ontario and provided much of the timber and rock for an international bridge that spanned the Rainy River at Baudette. Clementson served as a Beltrami County commissioner, with his district covering essentially what became Lake of the Woods County.

LEVI COOK
Died November 3, 1869, aged 42
**Greenfield Cemetery (also known as Cook's Valley Cemetery),
Kellogg, Wabasha County (Southern Region); old addition, block 5**

Levi Cook and his brother Aaron were the first white
settlers in the valley around what is now Kellogg.

LYMAN DAYTON
August 25, 1810–October 20, 1865
**Oakland Cemetery, St. Paul, Ramsey County
(Metro Region); block 26, lot 6**

Born to a wealthy
Connecticut family,
Lyman Dayton arrived
in Minnesota in 1849
and became a success-
ful land and railroad
speculator during the
next decade. He
owned land that
became known as
Dayton's Bluff to the
east of downtown St.
Paul, founded the city
of Dayton on the Mis-
sissippi River to the
northwest of Minne-
apolis, invested in

Lyman Dayton's grave marker, 2004

mills and water power, and was influential in the establishment of the Lake Superior and Mississippi Railroad,
serving as the railroad's president until his death in 1865.
Dayton was first buried on Dayton's Bluff but was re-
interred in Oakland Cemetery nearly four years later.

WILLIAM B. DODD
1811–August 23, 1862
Church of the Holy Communion, St. Peter,
Nicollet County (Southern Region)

The leader in the building of Dodd Road, a seventy-three-mile path constructed through the Big Woods in 1853 to connect Mendota to what is now St. Peter, William Dodd was a ferry boat operator, land speculator, and militia captain who was killed in New Ulm during the Dakota War.

MERTON EASTLICK
1851–November 13, 1875
Oakwood Cemetery, Rochester, Olmsted County
(Southern Region); section 1, lot 140, grave 7

Merton Eastlick, then eleven years old, rescued his infant brother after several members of his family, including his father, were killed and his mother wounded during the Dakota War. The Eastlicks, who had settled in Lake Shetek in southwestern Minnesota the year before, were fleeing the area when, at his mother's direction, Merton put his sixteen-month-old brother on his back and headed for Mankato. He was found after fifty miles and dubbed "The Boy Hero of Lake Shetek" by the press. After the war Merton and his mother, Lavina, traveled with a show depicting events of the conflict.

GURI ENDRESEN-ROSSELAND
March 26, 1813– June 20, 1881
Vikor Lutheran Church Cemetery, north of Willmar,
Kandiyohi County (Southern Region)

After her husband and one son were killed on August 21, 1862, during a Dakota War fight, Guri Endresen-Rosseland hid in the cellar of her home with her infant daughter. With her daughter and a son, who had been wounded, she later set out in an ox cart for Forest City, the nearest settlement, which was thirty miles away.

Along the way, she found two other settlers who had been wounded, taking them with her to the city.

PETE GAGNON
1847–June 14, 1935
Holy Rosary Catholic Church Cemetery, Grand Portage, Grand Portage Indian Reservation, Cook County (Northeast Region)

Gagnon was born and raised on the farm of his French-Canadian parents in Quebec. He arrived in Cook County in the 1890s and bought the only trading post in Grand Portage, which was located on an island in the bay. One of the few white men in this fur district, Gagnon conducted much of his business with Native American trappers. He was also one of the most successful commercial fishermen on the North Shore.

ARTHUR GAHBOW (WAWENABE)
April 26, 1935–April 11, 1991
Vineland Cemetery, Vineland, Mille Lacs County (North Central/West Region)

Son of artist *Batiste Sam,* Gahbow was the tribal chair of the Mille Lacs Band of Ojibwe during a significant period in Native American history. Gahbow, whose Ojibwe name of Wawenabe means "seated in a place of honor," served for nineteen years, beginning in 1972 and ending with his death. He took part in the "Trail of Broken Treaties," a protest march by Indians on the nation's capital in 1972 as well as the confrontation the following year between Native Americans and the federal government at Wounded Knee in South Dakota. Gahbow helped the Mille Lacs Band move closer to self-governance. During his tenure as chair, the band opened the Nay Ah Shing School, where reservation children could learn about their own history and language as well as subjects such as math and science. The opening of this school followed a walkout by children of the Mille Lacs Band from a public school in Onamia.

Gahbow also was involved in the establishment of Grand Casino Mille Lacs, which opened in 1991 and, along with Grand Casino Hinckley, allowed the Mille Lacs Band to return to economic self-sufficiency and rebuild its reservation.

ANDREW GOOD THUNDER (WAKINYANWASTE) & SNANA

Andrew Good Thunder, about 1815–February 15, 1901
**St. Cornelia's Episcopal Church, near Morton,
Redwood County (Southern Region)**

Snana, 1839–April 24, 1908
Santee Indian Reservation, Nebraska

Born and raised in Mendota, outside present-day St. Paul, Good Thunder went on many war parties against the Ojibwe, including three raids after the Battle of Pine Coulee in 1842. After the Dakota ceded their lands to the U.S. government through treaties in 1851, Good Thunder and his first wife, Snana, moved to the Dakota reservation near the Lower Sioux Agency. In 1861 Good Thunder became the first Dakota to be baptized, as Andrew, by Bishop *Henry Whipple,* who had first visited the agency the year before. The following year, with the outbreak of the Dakota War, Good Thunder fought in the battle at Fort Ridgely and distinguished himself with his bravery, according to Dakota leader *Jerome Big Eagle.* Good Thunder and Snana protected many of the white captives, with Snana taking particular care of *Mary Schwandt Schmidt.* Snana divorced Good Thunder in 1865 and later married Charles Brass at the Santee reservation in Nebraska, where she died. Good Thunder and his second wife, Sarah, later resumed farming at the Lower Sioux Agency. He donated a portion of his land for the rebuilding of the Episcopal mission, which became known as St. Cornelia's Church in honor of Bishop Whipple's first wife, Cornelia Wright Whipple, the original mission having been burned during the war. *(See portrait of Snana on page 75.)*

JOSEPH LAFRAMBOISE
1805–November 9, 1856
Fort Ridgely Cemetery, Fort Ridgely State Park and Historic Site, Nicollet County (Southern Region)

A fur trader and a member of a prominent mixed-blood family, LaFramboise served as an interpreter for treaties signed between the U.S. government and Dakotas in 1837 and 1851.

LAKE SHETEK SETTLERS
Died August 20, 1862
Lake Shetek State Park, Murray County (Southern Region)

A mass grave holds the remains of fifteen settlers killed at Lake Shetek on August 20, 1862, during the Dakota War. The six adults and nine children include one unknown twelve-year-old child as well as three members of the Eastlick family (*see Merton Eastlick*).

MARTIN LAYMAN & ELIZABETH LAYMAN
Martin Layman, January 18, 1811–July 25, 1886
Elizabeth Layman, died November 2, 1886, aged 73
Crystal Lake Cemetery, Minneapolis, Hennepin County (Metro Region); section 21, lot 18, Martin: grave 7, Elizabeth: grave 6

Born in Greene County, New York, Martin Layman arrived in Minnesota in 1853 and established a farmstead near what is now Lake Street and Cedar Avenue in south Minneapolis. He allowed a burial of the infant child of a fellow member of his church and as well as several more burials before formally establishing a cemetery. Officially Minneapolis Cemetery, it was known as Layman's Cemetery after the owners, who were buried in it. The cemetery was closed to burials in 1919 and many of the people interred, including Martin and Elizabeth Layman, were exhumed and re-interred in other cemeteries as the Layman's grandson hoped to develop the land. Before this could happen, the city bought out the Layman heir and has since maintained the property.

JAMES LYND
November 25, 1830–August 18, 1862
**Marker near Lower Sioux Agency,
Redwood County (Southern Region)**

A state senator in 1861, Lynd (his name is spelled Lynde on his grave marker) was a clerk at the store of Nathan and *Andrew Myrick* when he became first person killed at the Lower Sioux Agency at the outbreak of the Dakota War on August 18, 1862. A marker, on the south side of Redwood County Highway 2 to the west of Lower Sioux Agency State Historic Site, marks his supposed burial site. Whether or not Lynd's remains are at this spot, the marker is almost directly across the road from the site of the Myrick store.

MARPIYA OKI NAJIN (CUT NOSE)
Died December 26, 1862
Mdewakanton Repatriation Burial Site, near St. Cornelia's Episcopal Church, near Morton, Redwood County (Southern Region)

One of thirty-eight Dakota hanged by the federal government in Mankato for war crimes committed during the Dakota War, Chief Marpiya Oki Najin (Cut Nose) is buried with the repatriated remains of other Dakota who were forced from their homes during the war. As was common practice, local doctors took the bodies of Native Americans who had been hanged (sometimes digging them up after interment) for medical studies. Some sources say that Cut Nose's body was taken by Dr. William W. Mayo, whose sons, *Charles and William Mayo,* used the skeleton to learn osteology. Cut Nose was one of three Dakota hanged at Mankato whose bodies were eventually recovered and interred in the repatriation site.

MAZOMANI
About 1820–September 23, 1862
Upper Sioux Agency State Park, Yellow Medicine County (Southern Region)

Mazomani was among the Dakota leaders who participated in the 1858 treaty signing that ceded land on the
north side of the Minnesota River to the U.S. government. He was fatally wounded at the Battle of Wood
Lake, the closing battle of the Dakota War.

HAZEN MOOERS
August 3, 1789–April 3, 1858
**Fort Ridgely Cemetery, Fort Ridgely State Park and
Historic Site, Nicollet County (Southern Region)**

Mooers arrived in what became Minnesota in 1816 and
was a pioneer in the fur trade. He had a trading post at
Big Stone Lake for fifteen years before establishing a
new post near Fort Ridgely. In 1853 Mooers secured a
contract for erecting the first government buildings at
the Lower Sioux Agency.

ELIZA MÜLLER
April 21, 1831 or 1832–September 26, 1876
**Fort Ridgely Cemetery, Fort Ridgely State Park and Historic Site,
Nicollet County (Southern Region)**

The wife of the post surgeon at Fort Ridgely, Eliza
Müller not only helped care for the wounded during
the Dakota War, but also participated in the fighting,
helping to wheel a cannon into place and organizing
some of the refugees to produce musket ammunition.

ANDREW I. MYRICK
June 28, 1832–August 18, 1862
**Oakland Cemetery, St. Paul, Ramsey County
(Metro Region); block 3, lot 51**

Myrick operated a trading post at the Lower Sioux
Agency. He was unpopular with the Dakota for his refusal to extend credit to his customers when their an-
nuity payment from the federal government was late
and for his remark, "If they are hungry, let them eat

grass." When the Dakota War broke out at the Lower Agency, Myrick attempted to escape by jumping out a second-floor window of the store. He was shot and killed; later his body was found with his mouth stuffed with grass.

Andrew I. Myrick, about 1860

JOSEPH NAGANUB (SITS AHEAD)
1795–1894

Holy Family Cemeteries, Fond du Lac Indian Reservation, west of Cloquet, Carlton County (Northeast Region)

Naganub was one of the last of the Ojibwe chiefs of the Minnesota region and became the foremost spokesman for the Lake Superior bands, representing his people in numerous treaty negotiations in Washington, D.C., including the 1866 Treaty of Bois Forte that ceded the iron lands, which encompassed the Vermilion and Mesabi ranges in northeastern Minnesota, to the United States. There is some uncertainty about Naganub's year of birth; his grave marker gives it as 1795.

LIZZIE NAGANUB
Died October 1931, aged 82

Holy Family Cemeteries, Fond du Lac Indian Reservation, west of Cloquet, Carlton County (Northeast Region); unmarked grave

Daughter of *Joseph Naganub,* Lizzie Naganub was described as a "witch woman" on the White Earth Indian Reservation. She was buried in Holy Family Cemeteries, back on the Fond du Lac reservation, on October 7, 1931, and newspapers reported that a fiery ball (also described as an "apparition taking the form of an intermittent light") haunted her grave, bringing nightly visitors to the cemetery. The scientific explanation for the phenomenon was that such a light, often called a will-o'-the-wisp, was caused by bog gas. Some tribal members insisted that it was the result of Naganub being poisoned by a medicine man "whose powers were stronger than hers" and that the fireball was "a sort of proof to the tribesman that the woman was a victim of such a poison."

NA-MA-POCK
Died February 17, 1916
Indian Burial Grounds (formerly Highland Park Cemetery), on private property, Warroad, Roseau County (North Central/West Region)

According to his obituary, Na-Ma-Pock was camping at the mouth of the Warroad River at the time the international boundary between the United States and Canada was surveyed in 1874. He was from a tribal group led by his father and located on Buffalo Point, on the Canadian side of the border, but Na-Ma-Pock decided to stay on the U.S. side. When this land was ceded to the United States government, he was given an allotment. The traditional spirit house on Na-Ma-Pock's grave is one of four still existing on the grounds of a private home in Warroad. The others are for *John Ka-Ka-Gesick,* Little Thunder, and Laughing Mary.

EMILY PEAKE
May 28, 1920–April 18, 1995
St. Columba Mission, White Earth Indian Reservation, Becker County (North Central/West Region)

Emily Peake was a founding member and the executive director for seventeen years of the oldest Native American organization in Minneapolis, the Upper Midwest Native American Center. She was also a housing commissioner for the City of Minneapolis and a representative to the National Indian Council on Aging.

JEDEDIAH POPE
September 15, 1838–February 23, 1909
**Evergreen Cemetery, Caledonia, Houston County
(Southern Region); block D, lot 23, grave 1**

Pope was an early settler in Houston County, moving
with his parents in 1854 from Chautauqua County, New
York. During the Civil War, Pope enlisted in Company F
of the Twenty-third Illinois Infantry in Chicago. He became sick with the measles soon after joining up and left
the hospital without permission to join his company as
it was leaving for the front. After his discharge from the
army, Pope returned to his farm south of Caledonia,
where he lived and worked for nearly forty years before
selling the farm and moving into town.

PHILANDER PRESCOTT
September 17, 1801–August 18, 1862
**Minneapolis Pioneers and Soldiers Memorial
Cemetery (Layman's Cemetery), Hennepin County
(Metro Region); block A, lot 4, grave north end**

In 1819, following the death of his parents, Prescott left
his home in Ontario County, New York. Jobs as a sutler's
clerk eventually brought him to Minnesota, where he
went into business for himself, trading with Native
Americans along the Mississippi River. Prescott left Minnesota in the late 1820s but soon returned and became
an interpreter at Fort Snelling. He then taught methods
of European farming at a Native American farming community on the shores of Lake Calhoun. In August 1862
Prescott was an interpreter at Fort Ridgely on the Minnesota River when the Dakota War began. He fled the
agency and was on his way to Fort Ridgely when he was
killed by a party of Dakota. Prescott left behind his
Dakota wife and their children, as well as journals that
have become a valuable source of historical information
about the region, including the city of Prescott, Wisconsin, which is named after him.

MARY SCHWANDT SCHMIDT
March 23, 1848–July 26, 1939
**Oakland Cemetery, St. Paul, Ramsey County
(Metro Region); block 13, lot 45**

As a teenager, settler Mary Emilie Schwandt was captured on August 18, 1862, the first day of the Dakota War. Schwandt, who had several family members killed by the Dakota, was purchased from her captors by *Snana*, who protected her until the white captives were released. Schwandt later moved to St. Paul and married William Schmidt.

In 1899 old friends posed together when *Snana* (left) visited Mary Schwandt Schmidt in St. Paul.

TAOPI
About 1824–March 5, 1869

**Maple Lawn Cemetery, Faribault, Rice County
(Southern Region); section Q**

As the Battle of Wood Lake, the decisive battle in the
Dakota War, was being fought, Taopi was among a
group of Dakota who took charge of white and mixed-
blood captives and arranged for their safe release.

THOMAS WAKEMAN (WOWINAPE)
About 1846–January 13, 1886

**Redwood Falls Cemetery, Redwood Falls,
Redwood County (Southern Region); division 4**

Wowinape's role in the Dakota War is unclear, but he
may have been with his father, *Little Crow*, in the second battles at Fort Ridgely and New Ulm, and on the
expedition to the Big Woods. Present when Little Crow
was killed, Wowinape was later captured. In prison he
converted to Christianity and took the name Thomas
Wakeman. Eventually pardoned, he moved to Flandreau, Dakota Territory, where he founded the Dakota
Young Men's Christian Association.

EARTHLY CONCERNS

POLITICIANS, SUFFRAGISTS, LAWYERS, AND JUDGES

Although it is an intensely political state, Minnesota has never produced a U.S. president. It has contributed a pair of vice presidents (Hubert H. Humphrey and Walter Mondale) who ran for president, along with a pair of governors (John A. Johnson and Floyd B. Olson) who were considered presidential material but died early and in office.

Two of the state's most distinguished jurists—Harry Blackmun and Warren Burger—are buried elsewhere, in Arlington National Cemetery. Another, interred in Winona, is regarded as possibly the best judge in Minnesota history and is remembered today mainly because of his namesake, William Mitchell College of Law in St. Paul.

H. CARL ANDERSEN
January 27, 1897–July 26, 1978
Danebod Lutheran Cemetery, Tyler, Lincoln County (Southern Region); block G-2, lot 1

Andersen was a longtime member of the U.S. House of Representatives for Minnesota's Seventh Congressional District from 1939 to 1963. He was defeated in the Republican primary in 1962 after losing party support following his sale of shares in a coal mine to Texas millionaire Billy Sol Estes, who was convicted of fraud and theft for manipulating government programs.

EUGENIE MOORE ANDERSON
May 26, 1909–March 31, 1997
**Burnside Cemetery, Red Wing, Goodhue County
(Southern Region); lot 38, Old Section**

In 1949 Anderson became the first woman to serve as
a U.S. ambassador when President Harry S. Truman
appointed her ambassador to Denmark. In 1962, at the
height of the Cold War, Anderson was appointed as U.S.
minister to Bulgaria, thus becoming the first American
woman to serve as a chief of mission to an Eastern
European country. Anderson was influential in the
creation of the Democratic-Farmer-Labor party in Minnesota in the 1940s. In 1958 she campaigned unsuccessfully for the DFL nomination, won by Eugene
McCarthy, to the U.S. Senate.

JOHN BLATNIK
August 17, 1911–December 17, 1991
**Calvary Cemetery, Chisholm, St. Louis County
(Northeast Region); block H-1, lot 125**

Blatnik's first stint in politics, in the state Senate from
1941 to 1944, was spent mostly away from Minnesota
as he served with the Office of Strategic Services during
World War II, performing intelligence work for the military. Upon his discharge, Blatnik was elected to the
U.S. House of Representatives, representing his hometown of Chisholm in the Eighth Congressional District
until 1975.

GEORGE BRACKETT & MILLIE BRONSON
George Brackett, September 16, 1836–May 17, 1921
Millie Bronson,1770–March 7, 1885
**Lakewood Cemetery, Minneapolis, Hennepin County (Metro
Region); section 6, lot 260, Brackett: grave 17, Bronson: grave 22**

A supplier of food and transportation to Minnesota
units during the Civil War, mayor of Minneapolis, industrial empire builder, and one of the founders of

Lakewood Cemetery, Brackett is buried in the Brackett plot, along with Millie Bronson, a former slave known as Aunt Millie to the family. Major *Alfred Brackett,* a cousin of George's, hired Bronson to serve as his cook during the Civil War. When Alfred's cavalry company returned home on furlough in 1864, he left Bronson with George. According to one source, Bronson was "a servant of Confederate General Beauregard during the Civil War. She was captured at the Battle of Tishomingo by Major Brackett of St. Paul, and brought north to Minneapolis." Bronson was more than one hundred years old at the time of her death, according to the dates on her grave marker.

FANNY BRIN
October 20, 1884–
September 4, 1961
Adath-Yeshuran Cemetery, Edina, Hennepin County (Metro Region); section 2, block 1, lot 7, grave 5

Fanny Brin, about 1925

A worker for women's suffrage, teacher, and peace worker, the Romanian-born Brin was associated with Carrie Chapman Catt, who founded the National Committee on the Cause and Cure of War and was an alternate consultant to the United States delegation to the United Nations organizing conference in San Francisco in 1945. Brin was well regarded as a public speaker, a reputation she established, as Fanny Fligelman, while a student at the University of Minnesota in 1905 when she placed second in an oratorical contest that was won by *Theodore Christianson,* who later became governor of Minnesota.

PIERCE BUTLER
March 17, 1866–November 16, 1939
Calvary Cemetery, St. Paul, Ramsey County
(Metro Region); section 33, block 4

Butler was appointed to the United States Supreme Court in 1922 and served until his death. One of the "Four Horseman" in the 1930s—along with justices James McReynolds, George Sutherland, and Willis Van Devanter—Butler opposed every piece of New Deal legislation that came before him. Upon Butler's death, Chief Justice Charles Evans Hughes said, "Pierce Butler brought to this court not only his learning in the law but a rich store of practical experience."

SARAH COLVIN
September 12, 1865–April 22, 1949
Roselawn Cemetery, Roseville, Ramsey County
(Metro Region); division 9, lot 7

A nurse, author, and worker for women's suffrage—with the latter activity twice landing her in jail—Colvin was the founder of the Minnesota Congressional Union and a member of the state board of education from 1935 to 1941, when she resigned in protest over political control of that body.

BRIAN COYLE
June 25, 1944–August 23, 1991
Lakewood Cemetery, Minneapolis, Hennepin County
(Metro Region); section 55, lot 33, grave 4

Coyle was a community activist who served on the Minneapolis City Council from 1983 until his death in 1991 as a result of HIV. After an unsuccessful bid for the U.S. Senate in 1978, Coyle made his first run at the city council in 1981, losing by a narrow margin. He ran again two years later, outpolling five opponents in the primary and then winning the general election despite a late effort by some to discredit Coyle because he was gay. An advocate for the low-income communities of Minneapolis, Coyle pressed for money for urban renewal and renovation of deteriorating housing during his final year, when he was vice president of the council. Shortly before Coyle's death, the council approved his proposal to extend sick and bereavement leave to unmarried domestic partners of city employees.

EDWARD DEVITT
May 5, 1911–March 2, 1992
Resurrection Cemetery, Mendota Heights, Dakota County (Metro Region); section 13, lot 57, grave 3

A senior U.S. district judge, Devitt spent thirty-eight years on the federal bench and presided over many high-profile cases, including the 1961 racketeering trial of *Isadore "Kid Cann" Blumenfeld* and the 1963 fraud trial of former Minneapolis Mayor Marvin Kline. Devitt also served one term in Congress, in the 1940s, but was defeated in a 1948 reelection bid by Eugene McCarthy.

AUBREY DIRLAM
October 20, 1913–June 3, 1995
Redwood Falls Cemetery, Redwood Falls, Redwood County (Southern Region); division 8

Living on his family farm in Delhi, Minnesota, Dirlam served seventeen two-year terms in the Minnesota House of Representatives before retiring in 1975 and moving to Redwood Falls. In the House, Dirlam was minority and majority leader as well as speaker of the House. He was also instrumental in getting Southwest State University located in Marshall.

IGNATIUS DONNELLY
November 3, 1831–January 1, 1901
**Calvary Cemetery, St. Paul, Ramsey County,
(Metro Region); section 32, block 8, lot 2**

Known as "the Sage of Nininger," Donnelly was a lawyer,
farmer, statesman, orator, and author who became one
of the leading figures in the early history of Minnesota.
He was born in Philadelphia and was admitted to the
bar before arriving in 1856 in St. Paul, where he divided
his time between farming and literary pursuits in
Nininger, a village and steamboat landing upstream
from Hastings, where Donnelly purchased land and
built a large house with the expectation that the town
would grow and prosper. (Instead, it would wither away
following the economic panic of 1857.) Donnelly was
the state's lieutenant governor, commencing the mobi-
lization of Minnesota troops for the Civil War, before
being elected to the U.S. House of Representatives three
times. He was also a strong backer of women's suffrage
and anti-slavery movements, positions that may have
cost him his seat in Congress as he was drummed out
by the Republican leadership in Minnesota in 1869,
even though the masses within the party supported
him. Donnelly continued in politics, serving in the
Minnesota Senate and later running unsuccessfully to
regain his seat in Congress and for governor while also
researching the history of the lost civilization of Atlantis.
This resulted in his book *Atlantis: The Antediluvian
World,* which he followed up with several other books,
including one that revealed a cipher in Shakespeare's
works proving Francis Bacon's authorship, while also
starting a newspaper devoted to anti-monopoly princi-
ples. Donnelly just made it into the twentieth century,
dying during the late evening of January 1, 1901.

WALLACE DOUGLAS
September 21, 1852–December 8, 1930
**Prairie Home Cemetery, Moorhead, Clay County
(North Central/West Region); lot 5, first addition**

Douglas settled in Moorhead after he arrived in Minnesota in 1883. He served as city attorney and as county attorney for Clay County. Appointed to the Minnesota Supreme Court by Governor *Samuel Van Sant* on March 31, 1904, Douglas served barely nine months, retiring to return to private practice on January 1, 1905. He served on the state forestry board for more than twenty years and is credited with the preservation of Itasca State Park.

LEW DRILL
May 9, 1877–July 4, 1969
**Sunset Memorial Park, Minneapolis, Hennepin County
(Metro Region); block 8, section 348, grave 4**

A former major-league baseball player, Lew Drill served as United States district attorney for Minnesota in the late 1920s and early 1930s. Although his tenure was brief, it was eventful as he prosecuted (successfully) tycoon *Wilbur Foshay* for financial misdeeds and (unsuccessfully) gangster Roger Touhy and three others for the kidnapping of brewer *William Hamm Jr.* Drill was graduated from Hamline University in St. Paul in 1897 and then received a law degree from Georgetown University in Washington, D.C., where he was signed by the Senators as a catcher in 1902 and had two hits in his major-league debut in the season opener. He also played briefly that season for the Baltimore Orioles and later played for the Detroit Tigers. Drill came back to Minnesota and played for the minor league St. Paul Saints in 1906. Two years later he became athletics director at Hamline University while practicing law at the same time.

CHARLES E. FLANDRAU
July 15, 1828–September 9, 1903
**Oakland Cemetery, St. Paul, Ramsey County
(Metro Region); block 50, lot 18, grave 1**

A justice of the Minnesota territorial supreme court
in 1857 and 1858, Flandrau helped draft the first state
constitution and remained on the supreme court when
Minnesota achieved statehood in 1858, serving until
1864. During that time, he was also called upon to
recruit troops for the defense of New Ulm during the
Dakota War. Flandrau was a candidate for governor in
1867. He published numerous speeches as well as books
and encyclopedias on the history of Minnesota. Flandrau
State Park near New Ulm is named after him.

MELVIN GOLDBERG
April 27, 1942–August 30, 1998
**Minneapolis Jewish Cemetery, Richfield, Hennepin County
(Metro Region); section 2, block 3, lot 2**

Goldberg was a law professor at the University of Minnesota and a dean at the *William Mitchell* College of
Law who became nationally known for his work in
mental-health law and for his contributions to legal-aid
programs.

HAROLD HAGEN
November 10, 1901–March 19, 1957
**Oakdale Cemetery, Crookston, Polk County
(North Central/West Region)**

Hagen represented the Ninth Congressional District in
northwestern Minnesota for six terms beginning in 1943.
He was defeated in a reelection bid by *Coya Knutson* in
1954 and tried unsuccessfully to regain his seat two
years later, losing again to Knutson.

JEAN HARRIS
November 24, 1931–December 12, 2001
**Pleasant Hill Cemetery, Eden Prairie,
Hennepin County (Metro Region)**

The daughter of a doctor, Jean Harris grew up in a seg-
regated neighborhood in Richmond, Virginia, and followed her father into medicine while blazing new trails
for others to follow. In 1951 she became the first black
person admitted to the Medical College of Virginia. After
becoming a physician, Harris returned to the college as
its first black faculty member. She also found a niche in
politics and served in various capacities in several different presidential administrations before arriving in
Minnesota in the 1980s to be a vice president of government affairs for Control Data Corporation. Harris
was the running mate of Douglas Kelley when he unsuccessfully sought the Republican gubernatorial nomination in 1990. Five years later, Harris became mayor of
Eden Prairie, a post she held until her death.

GUY V. HOWARD
November 28, 1879–August 20, 1954
**Lakewood Cemetery, Minneapolis, Hennepin County
(Metro Region); section 8, lot 381, grave 6
(family monument; no individual marker)**

Guy Howard, the former head of the Minneapolis office
of the state's automobile license bureau, slipped into
the U.S. Senate for two months after discovering a quirk
in the election laws. Following the death in office of
Senator *Thomas Schall* in December 1935, with just over
a year left in his term, *Elmer Benson* was appointed to
fill the vacancy. Howard pointed out that Benson's appointment was effective only until the next election,
not until the new senator was sworn in, and filed to run
for the "short-term" Senate seat. Thus, in November
1936, two elections were held for the Minnesota seat in
the Senate. *Ernest Lundeen* won the "long-term" seat, but
Howard the "short-term" seat and went to Washington

as possibly the first senator ever elected to serve a non-existent term of Congress. He collected a salary and received a brass doorplate with his name on it before returning home. Harris tried the gambit four years later after Lundeen was killed in a plane crash but was unsuccessful. Then, in 1946, following the death of Minnesota Third District Representative William Gallagher, Howard won a write-in campaign to fill the two-month slot between the election and the swearing in of the new representative, but was refused a certificate by he state canvassing board.

HUBERT H. HUMPHREY & MURIEL HUMPHREY

Hubert H. Humphrey, May 27, 1911–January 13, 1978
Muriel Humphrey, February 20, 1912–September 20, 1998
Lakewood Cemetery, Minneapolis, Hennepin County (Metro Region); section 51, lot A, Hubert: grave 1, Muriel: grave 2

Minnesota's leading statesman, Hubert Horatio Humphrey was known as the "Happy Warrior" during his more than three decades of public service. Twice elected mayor of Minneapolis in the 1940s, Humphrey achieved national prominence with his oratory at the 1948 Democratic national convention that was instrumental in having President Harry S. Truman's civil rights proposals included in the party platform. He was elected to the U.S. Senate later that year and became a champion of liberal causes. After Lyndon B. Johnson became president, he selected Humphrey as his running mate in the 1964 election, which they won. When Johnson decided in 1968 not to run for another term, Humphrey announced his candidacy for president and received the Democratic nomination. Defeated by Richard Nixon in the general election, Humphrey then taught at Macalester College in St. Paul and returned to the Senate in 1971. Following his death from cancer in 1978, his widow, Muriel, assumed his Senate seat until a special election was held that fall. Muriel later married a childhood classmate, Max Brown; his surname also appears on her grave marker.

JANET JOHNSON
March 5, 1940–August 21, 1999
**Trinity Lutheran Church Cemetery, North Branch,
Chisago County (Metro Region)**

A legislator who was an advocate for environmental causes, Johnson was serving her third term in the state senate when she died of a brain tumor. With her husband, Dennis, Johnson founded Natural Spaces, a company that built geodesic dome houses. The Johnsons lived in such a home outside of North Branch.

MAGNUS JOHNSON
September 19, 1871–September 13, 1936
**Dassel Community Cemetery, Dassel, Meeker County
(Southern Region); block 3, section 2, lot 298, grave 2 1/2**

One of the organizers of the Farmer-Labor party in Minnesota, the colorful dirt farmer-politician from Meeker County represented Minnesota in the U.S. Senate and House of Representatives. While in Congress, he engaged in milking and woodchopping contests with Secretary of Agriculture Henry C. Wallace. Johnson's involvement in a marble-shooting contest with other senators prompted a letter from his wife, Har-

The grave marker for Magnus Johnson declares that the politician is "Going" to another meeting, 1997

riet, back in Minnesota, saying that if he didn't have anything better to do, he had better come home and

help her milk twenty cows. Born in Sweden and appren-
ticed to a glassblower, Johnson arrived in the United
States when he was nineteen years old and made his way
to Minnesota via New York and Wisconsin. He got involved in local politics while operating a farm in Kimball
and then won a seat in the state House of Representatives. He was defeated in a bid for governor by *J. A. O.
Preus* in 1922. The next year, however, he defeated Preus
in a special election to fill the remainder of the U.S. Senate term of *Knute Nelson,* who had died in office. Johnson was defeated in an election for a full term as well as
in another attempt to become governor. He returned to
Congress when the state's nine representatives were
elected at large in 1932; Johnson got the most votes of
the twenty-seven candidates in the election.

HAROLD KNUTSON
October 20, 1880–August 21, 1953
**North Star Cemetery, St. Cloud, Stearns County
(North Central/West Region); lot 319, grave 3**

Born in Norway, Knutson arrived in the United States
with his parents when he was six years old and later
owned several newspapers in central Minnesota. He
was elected to the U.S. House of Representatives and
served in Congress from 1917 to 1949, chairing the
House Ways and Means Committee during that time.

ODIN LANGEN
January 5, 1913–July 6, 1976
**Red River Lutheran Church Cemetery, Skane Township,
Kennedy, Kittson County (North Central/West Region)**

After eight years as a legislator in the Minnesota House
of Representatives, Langen started his career in Congress
by defeating two-time Representative *Coya Knutson* in a
campaign remembered largely for a plea from Knutson's
husband for Coya to come home. Langen served six

terms in the U.S. House of Representatives before being defeated in 1970 by Bob Bergland.

ERNEST LUNDEEN
August 4, 1878–August 31, 1940
Fort Snelling National Cemetery, Minneapolis, Hennepin County (Metro Region); section B, grave 140-S

A member of the Farmer-Labor party, Lundeen had served barely half of his term in the U.S. Senate when he was killed, along with twenty-four others, when his plane crashed in a field at the base of the Blue Ridge Mountains in Virginia. At the time, the death toll in the crash was the heaviest in the history of U.S. commercial aviation. Lundeen had served in the Twelfth Minnesota Volunteers during the Spanish-American War and later represented his state in the U.S. House of Representatives. Dogged by his vote against U.S. entry into World War I in 1917, Lundeen was defeated in a bid for reelection. In 1932 he returned to Congress, serving two terms in the House before being elected to the Senate.

FRED MARSHALL
March 13, 1906–June 5, 1985
Burr Oak Cemetery, Union Grove Township, Meeker County (Southern Region)

In his first try at elective office, Marshall unseated *Harold Knutson* in Minnesota's Sixth Congressional District in 1948. During his fourteen years in the U.S. House of Representatives, Marshall chaired the House Ways and Means Committee.

WILLIAM MITCHELL
November 19, 1832–August 21, 1900
**Woodlawn Cemetery, Winona,
Winona County (Southern Region);
section H, lot 36**

Born in Ontario and admitted to
the bar in Virginia, Mitchell later
settled in Minnesota and practiced law in Winona. Mitchell
was a member of the Winona city
council, a county attorney, and a
representative in the Minnesota

William Mitchell, about 1870

legislature. He was elected district judge in 1874 and
then served on the Minnesota Supreme Court from
1881 to 1899, originally being appointed by Governor
John S. Pillsbury. He was later elected to a full term and
eventually defeated in a reelection bid. Regarded as one
of the greatest judges in the history of the state, Mitchell
was the choice of the St. Paul College of Law to be the
school's first dean. He died unexpectedly, however, in
August 1900. In 1956, when the St. Paul College of Law
merged with the Minneapolis-Minnesota College of
Law, the resulting school in St. Paul was named the
William Mitchell College of Law in his honor.

DORILUS MORRISON
December 27, 1814–June 26, 1897
**Lakewood Cemetery, Minneapolis, Hennepin County
(Metro Region); section 2, lot 35, grave 3.5**

Morrison was one of the pioneers of Minneapolis, serving
as its first mayor in 1867 when the town was upgraded to
a city by a charter issued by the state legislature. Morrison
served two different stints as mayor, the latter covering a
ten-year period that included the 1872 merging of Minneapolis with St. Anthony, which had been an independent
city on the east bank of the Mississippi River. A native of
Maine, Morrison was involved in numerous enterprises,
including banking and milling.

WILLARD MUNGER
January 20, 1911–July 11, 1999
Oneota Cemetery, Duluth, St. Louis County
(Northeast Region); 2nd division of O, lot 68, grave 2

Munger was known as "Mr. Environment" for his advocacy of environmental causes during his more than forty years in the Minnesota legislature, representing the Duluth area. He successfully fought for restrictions on the pesticide DDT in 1969, establishment of the Environmental and Natural Resources Trust Fund in 1990, and the converting of abandoned railroad rights-of-way into state trails. A sixty-nine-mile bicycle trail from Hinckley to Duluth bears his name. When he died, while still in office at the age of eighty-eight, he was the oldest state legislator in Minnesota history.

ANCHER NELSEN
October 11, 1904–November 30, 1992
Oakland Cemetery, Hutchinson, McLeod County
(Southern Region); northwest corner of cemetery

Nelsen's career in politics spanned forty years, starting with service in the Minnesota Senate in the 1930s and finishing with sixteen years in the U.S. House of Representatives. In between, Nelson chaired the Republican Farm Platform Committee, was an agricultural adviser in Dwight D. Eisenhower's presidential campaign, and served as administrator of the Rural Electrification Administration. Nelsen was a Minnesota lieutenant governor and also an unsuccessful candidate for governor, losing to *Orville Freeman* in 1956.

ARTHUR NELSON
May 10, 1892–April 11, 1955
Oakland Cemetery, St. Paul, Ramsey County
(Metro Region); block 45, lot 128

In 1936 *Guy V. Howard* exploited a flaw in Minnesota election law that made an appointment to a Congressional vacancy good only until the next election. The state legislature eventually modified the law to make the appointment good until the next elected senator or representative took office. Before this happened, however, the situation arose again. Joseph Ball was appointed to fill the vacancy in the U.S. Senate created by the death of *Ernest Lundeen*. Ball ran for and won a full term in 1942 but would not take office until January 6. As was the case in 1936, two senate elections were held, one for the long term and the other for the short term. This time, former St. Paul mayor Arthur Nelson won the short-term election and held a spot in the Senate between the two terms—one appointed and one elected—by Ball.

ANNA DICKIE OLESEN
July 3, 1885–May 21, 1971
**Sakatah Cemetery, Waterville, Le Sueur County
(Southern Region); lot 340, grave 5**

After finally becoming eligible to vote at the age of thirty-five, following the ratification of the Nineteenth Amendment to the U.S. Constitution, the eloquent Welsh American Olesen was a Minnesota delegate to the Democratic national convention in 1920 and a candidate for the U.S. Senate two years later, easily defeating two other candidates in the primary election before finishing third to *Henrik Shipstead* and Frank B. Kellogg in the general election.

Anna Dickie Olesen, about 1920

EDMUND RICE
February 14, 1819–July 11, 1889
**Oakland Cemetery, St. Paul, Ramsey County
(Metro Region); block 3, lot 44**

After serving as assistant quartermaster with Company A of the Michigan Volunteers during the Mexican War, Rice arrived in St. Paul in 1849 and became a pioneer in the railroad business of the Northwest. A younger brother of *Henry Mower Rice,* he also was a member of the House of Representatives in both Minnesota's territorial and state legislatures. Rice was unsuccessful in his bid to be elected governor in 1879, but he followed up by becoming mayor of St. Paul and later the state's Fourth District Representative in Congress.

HENRY MOWER RICE
November 29, 1816–January 15, 1894
**Oakland Cemetery, St. Paul, Ramsey County
(Metro Region); block 25, lot 1**

As a fur trader after arriving in Minnesota in 1839, Rice secured the trust of the Ojibwe and was instrumental in negotiating the treaty between the Ojibwe and U.S. government in 1847. An adept lobbyist and persuader, he worked to establish the Minnesota Territory and served as the territory's delegate from 1853 to 1857. Following statehood, Minnesota was represented by Rice in the U.S. Senate from 1858 to 1863. Rice also was a member of the board of regents from 1851 to 1859 and was president of the Minnesota Historical Society. As a United States Commissioner, Rice continued to negotiate treaties with the Indians in the 1880s.

THOMAS SCHALL
June 4, 1878–December 22, 1935
**Lakewood Cemetery, Minneapolis,
Hennepin County (Metro Region);
section 44, lot 140B, grave 2**

Thomas Schall, 1918

A vigorous critic of the New
Deal, Schall was a skilled orator
known for his vitriolic attacks
on Franklin and Eleanor Roosevelt from the floor of the U.S.
Senate in the 1930s. Victim of
an electric shock that paralyzed
his optic nerve in 1907, Schall
was, along with Senator Thomas Gore of Oklahoma,
one of the very few blind persons ever to serve in
Congress. After five terms in the House of Representatives, Schall was elected to the Senate in 1924 and
reelected six years later. Schall was anticipating a strong
challenge from *Floyd B. Olson,* then Minnesota's governor, in his bid for a third term. Neither man made it to
the election, however. In December 1935 Schall was
struck by an automobile outside of Washington, D.C.,
and died a few days later. Olson died of cancer the
following August.

CHARLES W. SCRUTCHIN
September 11, 1866–July 14, 1930
**Greenwood Cemetery, Bemidji, Beltrami County
(North Central/West Region); block 1, lot 3 S 1/2**

Scrutchin was an African American lawyer who arrived in
Minnesota in 1898 and began
practicing law in Bemidji. In
1920 Scrutchin represented
William Miller, one of a number of black circus workers ac-

Charles W. Scrutchin, about 1910

cused of rape in Duluth, an incident that resulted in the lynching by a white mob of three of the men (*see Duluth lynching victims*). Scrutchin was able to get Miller acquitted, a verdict that also resulted in the dismissal of charges against the other defendants.

HENRIK SHIPSTEAD
January 8, 1881–June 26, 1960
Kinkead Cemetery, Alexandria, Douglas County (North Central/West Region); addition 1, division 10, block 4, lot 6, grave 1

In 1922 Shipstead became the first member of the Farmer-Labor party to be elected to the U.S. Senate from Minnesota. He served four terms, switching to the Republican party during his tenure. An isolationist, Shipstead was against U.S. involvement in World War II although he voted for a declaration of war following the bombing of Pearl Harbor. After the war, Shipstead was one of only two senators to vote against ratification of the United Nations. He was defeated by Governor *Edward Thye* for the Republican nomination for the Senate in 1946 after waging his campaign on his opposition to U.S. participation in the UN.

LENA O. SMITH
August 13, 1885–November 6, 1966
Lakewood Cemetery, Minneapolis, Hennepin County (Metro Region); section 22, lot 341, grave 4

Also educated as a hairdresser and an embalmer, Smith was the first black woman lawyer in Minnesota and reportedly the first in the country west of Washington, D.C. She was also the first woman president of the Minneapolis Chapter of the National Association for the Advancement of Colored People and a founding member of the Minneapolis Urban League in 1925.

HALVOR STEENERSON
June 30, 1852–November 22, 1926
**Oakdale Cemetery, Crookston, Polk County
(North Central/West Region); division F, block 1**

Serving twenty years in the U.S. House of Representatives, Steenerson chaired the Post Office and Post Roads
Committee, which established and developed the Rural
Free Delivery service. Steenerson lived in Crookston from
1880 until his death forty-six-and-a-half years later.

JAMES A. TAWNEY
January 3, 1855–June 12, 1919
**Woodlawn Cemetery, Winona, Winona County
(Southern Region); section H, lot 75, grave 6**

A blacksmith who arrived in Winona in 1877, Tawney
received his law degree in 1882 and entered politics
eight years later. After one term in the Minnesota Sen-
ate, he was elected to Congress and served nine terms.
He was known as "The Watchdog of the United States
Treasury" while chairing the House Appropriations
Committee. He was also a member of the International
Joint Commission, which produced a report on pollu-
tion of boundary waters. He was the father of soldier
James Millard Tawney.

HENRY "TYPHOID" TRUELSEN
October 20, 1844–December 3, 1931
**Forest Hill Cemetery, Duluth, St. Louis County
(Northeast Region); section D, block 1, lot 6**

Henry Truelsen was elected mayor of Duluth in 1896
after fighting successfully against the city's purchase of
the local drinking water system, which was then pri-
vately owned. A boom town at the time, Duluth had
an expanding population that stretched the capacity of
its waterworks, and typhoid was rampant within the
city. Truelsen's work to defeat an 1894 referendum that
would have purchased the system for $2 million delayed

the city's acquisition of the utility and resulted in his being nicknamed "Typhoid" Truelsen by the current mayor. After Truelsen was elected, the city purchased the water works for $1.25 million. Truelsen was re-elected in 1898 but was defeated by five votes in his bid for a third term two years later.

CLARA UELAND
October 10, 1860–March 1, 1927
Lakewood Cemetery, Minneapolis, Hennepin County (Metro Region); section 9, lot 208, grave 3

Ueland was president of the Minnesota Woman Suffrage Association from 1914 to 1919 and then became the first president of the Minnesota League of Women Voters. She also established the Minneapolis Kindergarten Association and was a member of the first governing board of the state art commission.

BRUCE VENTO
October 7, 1940–October 10, 2000
Forest Lawn Memorial Park, Maplewood, Ramsey County (Metro Region); block 32-D, lot 145, grave 3

Vento was raised on St. Paul's East Side and served three terms in the state legislature before being elected to the U.S. House of Representatives in 1976. An advocate for the homeless as well as for the environment, Vento was honored by the Sierra Club and received the Conservationist of the Year Award for 1987 from the National Parks Conservation Association. Vento served nearly twenty-four years in Congress, retiring after being diagnosed with lung cancer, which was apparently brought on by exposure to asbestos during his earlier years as a laborer. Vento eventually died from the disease, but not before being instrumental in bringing about federal legislation granting U.S. citizenship to many Hmong American people who had fought for the United States during the Vietnam War.

ANDREW VOLSTEAD
October 31, 1859–January 20, 1947
Granite Falls Cemetery, Granite Falls, Minnesota,
Chippewa County (Southern Region); block 5, lot 2

Unfortunately best known for the Volstead Act—the
enactment of legislation for the U.S. Constitution's
Eighteenth Amendment that banned the manufacture,
sale, and distribution of intoxicating liquors until it
was repealed fourteen years later—Andrew Volstead
served ten terms in the U.S. House of Representatives,
representing west-central Minnesota. In Congress
Volstead chaired the Committee on the Judiciary and
argued for enactment of federal legislation to outlaw
lynchings. He also coauthored the Capper-Volstead Act,
which enabled farmers to form cooperatives without
being prosecuted under the Sherman Antitrust Act.

PAUL WELLSTONE
July 21, 1944–October 25, 2002
Lakewood Cemetery, Minneapolis, Hennepin County
(Metro Region); section 1, lot 13, grave 3

The man who said he would stand up for "the little
fellers, not the Rockefellers" represented Minnesota in
the U.S. Senate from 1991 to 2002. Wellstone arrived
in Minnesota in 1969 to teach at Carleton College in
Northfield. He ran unsuccessfully for state auditor
in 1982 but remained active in politics. In 1990 he received the Democratic-Farmer-Labor endorsement and
nomination for the U.S. Senate and then upset incumbent Rudy Boschwitz in the general election. Wellstone
held his seat by defeating Boschwitz again in 1996 and
ran for a third term in 2002. Eleven days before the
election, Wellstone was on his way to a funeral, while
preparing for a debate later in the day, when his plane
crashed near Eveleth. Wellstone was killed along with
seven others, including three staff members as well as
his wife, Sheila, and daughter, Marcia Markuson.

GRAVE AUTHORITY

MINNESOTA'S GOVERNORS

Oakland Cemetery in St. Paul was *the* burial spot for many of Minnesota's early governors, but Lakewood Cemetery in Minneapolis took the lead in 2003 with the interment there of Orville Freeman. Each cemetery had one who got away. Cushman Davis was buried at Oakland but is now in Arlington National Cemetery in Virginia. Lucius Hubbard was interred at Lakewood but reburied in Red Wing following the death of his wife ten years later. There is even a bit of mystery regarding a couple of governors. It is often reported that Winfield Scott Hammond either is or has been interred at Oakland. Neither is true. He was buried at Mount Hope Cemetery in St. James right after his death. Adolph Eberhart is listed by some sources as being in a family plot in Chicago, although he is in Lakewood.

TERRITORIAL GOVERNORS

Minnesota Territory was created by the United States Congress on March 3, 1849.

ALEXANDER RAMSEY
1ST TERRITORIAL GOVERNOR, 1849–53
September 8, 1815–April 22, 1903
Oakland Cemetery, St. Paul, Ramsey County
(Metro Region); block 15, lot 1

A Pennsylvania lawyer, Ramsey was appointed by President Zachary Taylor as Minnesota's first territorial governor. Ramsey remained in St. Paul and, as the second governor of the state (*see* page 101), was in Washington, D.C., in time to offer the first Union troops to President

Abraham Lincoln for the Civil War. He represented
Minnesota in the U.S. Senate from 1863 to 1875 and
later was secretary of war under Rutherford B. Hayes.
Ramsey was one of only two Minnesota governors
(*Orville Freeman* being the other) to serve as a member
of a presidential cabinet.

WILLIS GORMAN
2ND TERRITORIAL GOVERNOR, 1853–57
January 12, 1816–May 20, 1876
**Oakland Cemetery, St. Paul, Ramsey County
(Metro Region); block 20, lot 1**

Gorman, a native of Kentucky, was appointed governor
by President Franklin Pierce. Remaining in Minnesota
to practice law, Gorman later organized and commanded
the First Minnesota Volunteer Infantry Regiment in the
Civil War.

SAMUEL MEDARY
3RD TERRITORIAL GOVERNOR, 1857–58
February 25, 1801–November 7, 1864
Green Lawn Cemetery, Columbus, Ohio

An Ohio journalist who was appointed governor of the
Minnesota Territory by President James Buchanan,
Medary served less than a year, returning to Ohio
shortly before Minnesota achieved statehood in 1858.

STATE GOVERNORS

Minnesota became the thirty-second state of the United States of America on May 11, 1858.

HENRY H. SIBLEY
1ST STATE GOVERNOR,
1858–60
February 20, 1811–
February 18, 1891
Oakland Cemetery, St. Paul, Ramsey County (Metro Region); block 16, lot 2

Henry H. Sibley, about 1865

Sometimes called "the princely pioneer," Sibley arrived in Minnesota from Detroit in 1834 to work as a fur trader stationed in Mendota. As a delegate to the U.S. Congress, representing what was then a part of the Wisconsin Territory, Henry Hastings Sibley supported the act that organized Minnesota Territory in 1849. When the territory achieved statehood nine years later, Sibley was elected the first governor of the state. In between, Sibley was present at treaty signings that the federal government held with various bands of Dakota in order to purchase much of the land in Minnesota west of the Mississippi River. In 1862, after the Dakota rebelled against the U.S. government and killed settlers in areas along the Minnesota River, Governor *Alexander Ramsey* commissioned Sibley as a colonel and put him in charge of a state military expedition. The six-week war ended following a victory by Sibley's troops in the Battle of Wood Lake on September 23.

ALEXANDER RAMSEY
1ST TERRITORIAL GOVERNOR (*see* pages 99–100) &
2ND STATE GOVERNOR, 1860–63

HENRY SWIFT
3RD STATE GOVERNOR, 1863–64
March 23, 1823–February 25, 1869
Maple Grove Cemetery, Ravenna, Ohio

After studying law, Swift arrived in St. Paul in 1853 and three years later helped to found the city of St. Peter, where he lived for the rest of his life. He is buried in his Ohio birthplace.

STEPHEN MILLER
4TH STATE GOVERNOR, 1864–66
January 7, 1816–August 18, 1881
Worthington Cemetery, Worthington, Nobles County (Southern Region)

Miller was a lieutenant colonel in the First Minnesota Volunteer Infantry Regiment and saw action in the first battle of Manassas (Bull Run) during the Civil War. He was promoted to colonel in the Seventh Minnesota and, after taking over command from *Henry H. Sibley,* was placed in charge of prisoners from the Dakota War in Minnesota and handled the details of the hanging of thirty-eight convicted Dakota in December 1862. Miller was elected governor in Minnesota in 1863 and was occupied with securing Minnesota recruits for the Union army.

WILLIAM R. MARSHALL
5TH STATE GOVERNOR, 1866–70
October 17, 1825–January 8, 1896
Oakland Cemetery, St. Paul, Ramsey County (Metro Region); block 5, circle E & H

Riding his horse *Don,* Marshall rose to the rank of brevet brigadier general during the Civil War and was a lieutenant colonel in the Seventh Minnesota Volunteer Infantry Regiment, which was sent back to Minnesota during the Dakota War of 1862. A strong advocate of education, particularly for children of settlers across the state, Marshall had served in the territorial legislature and later became governor.

HORACE AUSTIN
6TH STATE GOVERNOR, 1870–74
October 15, 1831–November 7, 1905
Oakland Cemetery, St. Paul, Ramsey County (Metro Region); block 41, lot 17

Austin initially received the Republican nomination for governor because of qualities he shared with *Ignatius Donnelly*. Although Donnelly had been dumped by state Republican leaders, at the convention it was determined that a candidate similar to Donnelly was necessary out of fear of a split within the party that would result in the Democrats winning the gubernatorial race. Austin still won by only a narrow margin. He served two terms, and during his administration, the first geological survey, by the University of Minnesota, was done to determine the extent of the state's natural resources, a study that revealed the low-grade ore and taconite in northeastern Minnesota—a harbinger of riches to come. A New England native, Austin had arrived in Minnesota in 1856. He enlisted in the St. Peter Frontier Guard and took part in the defense of New Ulm during the Dakota War of 1862.

CUSHMAN DAVIS
7TH STATE GOVERNOR, 1874–76
June 16, 1838–November 27, 1900

Minnesota's U.S. senator from 1887 until his death, Davis was buried in Oakland Cemetery in St. Paul but was reinterred in Arlington National Cemetery in Arlington, Virginia.

JOHN S. PILLSBURY
8TH STATE GOVERNOR, 1876–82
June 29, 1827–October 18, 1901
Lakewood Cemetery, Minneapolis, Hennepin County
(Metro Region); section 2, lot 285, grave 3

A businessman, Pillsbury was the first Minnesota governor without military experience and the first to serve three terms. He was also the first of the Pillsbury family to locate in St. Anthony (now part of Minneapolis), in 1855. He became associated with his nephew, Charles A. Pillsbury, in the milling business. While his relatives built the Pillsbury Company, John Pillsbury is better remembered as the first major benefactor of the University of Minnesota.

LUCIUS HUBBARD
9TH STATE GOVERNOR, 1882–87
January 26, 1836–February 5, 1913
Oakwood Cemetery, Red Wing, Goodhue County (Southern
Region); block D, lot 30, section 6 (on Hubbard Ave.,
north of Summit Ave., within cemetery)

Born in Troy, New York, Hubbard arrived in Red Wing in 1857 and started the *Red Wing Republican* newspaper. He also engaged in the grain and milling business. In 1861 Hubbard joined the Fifth Minnesota Volunteer Infantry Regiment and rose to the rank of brigadier general. He was also a general in the Spanish-American War. In between, Hubbard served as governor. He was originally buried in Lakewood Cemetery in Minneapolis, but was reinterred in Red Wing following the death of his wife, Amelia, in 1923.

ANDREW MCGILL
10TH STATE GOVERNOR, 1887–89
February 19, 1840–October 31, 1905
Oakland Cemetery, St. Paul, Ramsey County
(Metro Region); block 35, lot 100

Shortly after arriving in St. Peter, where he studied law, McGill enlisted in the Ninth Minnesota Volunteer Infantry Regiment, which saw action in Minnesota during the Dakota War of 1862. During his tenure as governor, he oversaw the establishment of the Minnesota Soldiers Home for military veterans and the equalization of the school burden among districts in the state.

WILLIAM MERRIAM
11TH STATE GOVERNOR, 1889–93
July 26, 1849–February 18, 1931
Rock Creek Cemetery, Washington, D.C.

Governor of Minnesota from 1889 to 1893 and later director of the United States census under President William McKinley, Merriam never returned to Minnesota after federal service, remaining in Washington, D.C.

KNUTE NELSON
12TH STATE GOVERNOR, 1893–95
February 2, 1842 (marker says 1843)–April 28, 1923
**Kinkead Cemetery, Alexandria, Douglas County
(North Central/West Region); original addition,
division H, block 8, lot south 1/2, grave 2**

Serving from 1893 to 1895, Nelson was the first Minnesota governor to reflect the large wave of Scandinavian immigration in the state. Born in Norway, Nelson was living in Wisconsin when he enlisted in a Union regiment of his countrymen to fight in the Civil War. Wounded and captured, Nelson was released in a prisoner exchange and returned to his regiment. After serving in the Wisconsin assembly, Nelson arrived in Minnesota in 1871 and established a law practice. He served in the Minnesota Senate and in 1882 defeated Charles Kindred of Brainerd in a bitter election to represent Minnesota in the new Congressional district on the Dakota border. Nelson served three terms in the U.S. House of Representatives and became governor of

Minnesota in 1893. Shortly into his second term, in 1895, Nelson left the governorship to become a U.S. senator. He served in the Senate until his death during a train journey in 1923.

DAVID CLOUGH
13TH STATE GOVERNOR, 1895–99
December 27, 1846–August 28, 1924
Evergreen Cemetery, Everett, Washington

Clough arrived in Minnesota in 1857 and later established a successful lumber business in Minneapolis. After serving as a state senator, lieutenant governor, and governor, he moved to Washington state, still engaged with lumber.

JOHN LIND
14TH STATE GOVERNOR, 1899–1901
March 25, 1854–September 18, 1930
Lakewood Cemetery, Minneapolis, Hennepin County
(Metro Region); section 10, lot 204, grave 3

Born in Sweden, Lind was governor of Minnesota from 1899 to 1901 after serving in the U.S. Army during the Spanish-American War. As a member of the Democrat-Populist party, Lind ended a reign of Republican Minnesota governors that went back to *Alexander Ramsey*, defeating former Minneapolis mayor William Eustis. Lind also represented Minnesota in the U.S. House of Representatives before and after his term as governor.

SAMUEL VAN SANT
15TH STATE GOVERNOR, 1901–5
May 11, 1844–October 3, 1936
Glendale Cemetery, LeClaire, Iowa.

Speaker of the Minnesota House of Representatives and governor from 1901 to 1905, Van Sant was the last Minnesota governor who had served in the Civil War.

JOHN A. JOHNSON
16TH STATE GOVERNOR, 1905–9
July 28, 1861–September 21, 1909

Greenhill Cemetery, St. Peter, Nicollet County
(Southern Region); southeast section, lot 47, grave 3

Born near the village of Traverse des Sioux and raised in St. Peter, where he later was the editor and part owner of the *St. Peter Herald,* Johnson became in 1905 the first Minnesota-born governor of the state. He sought the Democratic nomination for president in 1908 but lost to William Jennings Bryan. It was thought Johnson would be the leading candidate for the nomination in 1912, but he died while still governor in 1909.

ADOLPH EBERHART
17TH STATE GOVERNOR, 1909–15
June 23, 1870–December 6, 1944

Lakewood Cemetery, Minneapolis, Hennepin County
(Metro Region); section 5, lot 252, grave 4

A Swedish immigrant, Eberhart became governor upon the death in office of *John A. Johnson* in 1909. He served the remainder of Johnson's term, then was elected to two more two-year terms. Eberhart helped to bring an end to capital punishment in Minnesota and oversaw legislation to create a statewide direct primary election, which was used for the first time in 1912. In 1914, rather than run for another term as governor, Eberhart sought the Republican nomination for the U.S. Senate and was defeated by Frank B. Kellogg.

WINFIELD SCOTT HAMMOND
18TH STATE GOVERNOR, 1915–15
November 17, 1863–December 30, 1915

Mount Hope Cemetery, St. James,
Watonwan County (Southern Region)

Hammond served less than a year as governor of Minnesota before dying in December 1915. He was the second of three Minnesota governors to die in office (*John A. Johnson* in 1909 and *Floyd B. Olson* in 1936 being the others). Hammond represented Minnesota in the U.S. House of Representatives before becoming governor. He died in Louisiana; his remains were brought back to Minnesota and buried in St. James. Although it is sometimes reported that he was interred in Oakland Cemetery in St. Paul, this alleged burial never took place.

J. A. A. BURNQUIST
19TH STATE GOVERNOR, 1915–21
July 21, 1879–January 12, 1961

Lakewood Cemetery, Minneapolis, Hennepin County
(Metro Region); section 27, lot 717, grave 3

After serving in the Minnesota House of Representatives and as lieutenant governor, Joseph Alfred Arner Burnquist became governor upon the death of *Winfield Scott Hammond* in 1915 and remained in office until 1921. Burnquist was later the state's attorney general from 1939 to 1955. *(See portrait on page 174.)*

J. A. O. PREUS
20TH STATE GOVERNOR, 1921–25
August 28, 1883–May 24, 1961

Lutheran Cemetery, Decorah, Iowa

Jacob Aall Ottesen Preus, a lawyer and businessman, was also state insurance commissioner and state auditor.

THEODORE CHRISTIANSON
21ST STATE GOVERNOR, 1925–31
September 12, 1883–December 10, 1948

Sunset Memorial Park, Minneapolis, Hennepin County
(Metro Region); Community Mausoleum, Chapel Level,
corridor 4, section 5, tier D

A lawyer and newspaper publisher, Christianson sandwiched in three terms as Minnesota governor, between

1925 and 1931 and between ten years in the Minnesota House of Representatives and four years in the U.S. House. Running for the U.S. Senate in 1936, he was defeated by *Ernest Lundeen.* Christianson authored a five-volume history of Minnesota.

FLOYD B. OLSON
22ND STATE GOVERNOR, 1931–36
November 13, 1891–August 22, 1936

Lakewood Cemetery, Minneapolis, Hennepin County (Metro Region); section 18, lot 113, grave 2

Raised in a working-class family in north Minneapolis, the charismatic Floyd Bjornstjerne Olson worked at laboring jobs in the Pacific Northwest and was a member of the International Workers of the World (the radical Wobblies) before returning to Minnesota, where he attended law school and was admitted to

Floyd B. Olson with a young 4-H Club member promoting potatoes grown in Minnesota's Arrowhead area, about 1934

the bar. He entered politics as part of the Committee of 48 to persuade Robert La Follette to run for president as a Progressive in 1920. Olson became Hennepin County attorney and earned the respect of local labor leaders by prosecuting corrupt members of the Citizens Alliance, an association committed to the open shop. He unsuccessfully sought the Democratic nomination for the U.S. House of Representatives, and, in 1924, was defeated in his first bid for governor as member of the Farmer-Labor party. Six years later, however, Olson became the first member of that party to be elected governor. True to his earlier career as a longshoreman in the West, he continued fighting on behalf of farmers, small business operators, and laborers, especially by his refusal to call in state troops to stop strikes in Minneapolis (truckers) and Austin (meatpackers). Olson was twice reelected governor and received the Farmer-Labor nomination for the U.S. Senate in 1936. It was widely thought he would make a run for the White House four years later. Olson was already suffering from stomach cancer, however, and died at the early age of forty-four.

HJALMAR PETERSEN
23RD STATE GOVERNOR, 1936–37
January 2, 1890–March 29, 1968
Bethlehem Lutheran Cemetery, Askov, Pine County (Northeast Region)

Born in Denmark, Petersen founded the *Askov American* in 1914 and served as the editor and publisher of this newspaper serving the Danish community in central Minnesota. An accomplished violinist, Petersen was the leader of a small orchestra that played at area dances and was director of the Askov community band. Petersen also had a strong interest in government and was elected to the Minnesota House of Representatives in 1930. He became lieutenant governor in 1935 and ascended to the governorship following the death in office of *Floyd B. Olson* the following year. Petersen did not seek a full term as governor and instead was elected railroad and warehouse commissioner.

ELMER BENSON
24TH STATE GOVERNOR, 1937–39
September 22, 1895–March 13, 1985
Appleton Cemetery, Appleton, Swift County (North Central/ West Region); Original Cemetery, block 27, section 2

A self-described "radical" who was characterized as a Communist sympathizer during his reelection campaign for governor in 1938, Benson was voted out of the governor's office by the largest margin in Minnesota history, receiving only 34 percent of the votes and losing to *Harold Stassen* in 1938. A member of the Farmer-Labor party, Benson had been appointed by Governor *Floyd B. Olson* to fill the vacancy in the U.S. Senate created by the death of *Thomas Schall* in late 1935, with the understanding that Benson would run for governor in 1936, leaving the Farmer-Labor nomination for the Senate seat open for a bid by Olson. Benson was elected governor, but Olson died before the Senate election.

HAROLD STASSEN
25TH STATE GOVERNOR, 1939–43
April 13, 1907–March 4, 2001

Acacia Park Cemetery, Mendota Heights, Dakota County (Metro Region); Cedar section, block 18, lot A, grave 4

Best known for the persistent presidential campaigns, most of which he considered symbolic, that caused his name to become a catchphrase for political futility, Stassen had a distinguished career in Minnesota politics. He was elected governor, in 1938, at the age of thirty-one and was twice reelected. He resigned in 1943 to serve as the chief of staff to Admiral William Halsey in the South Pacific. Following World War II, Stassen was part of the U.S. delegation to the original United Nations charter meetings in San Francisco in 1945. He made his strongest presidential bid in 1948, losing the Republican nomination to Thomas Dewey. Stassen followed with eight more presidential candidacies, the last one in 1992, and also ran unsuccessfully for the U.S. Senate, governor of Minnesota and of Pennsylvania (Stassen was president of the University of Pennsylvania from 1948 to 1953), and mayor of Philadelphia.

EDWARD J. THYE
26TH STATE GOVERNOR, 1943–47
April 26, 1896–August 28, 1969
Oaklawn Cemetery, Northfield, Rice County
(Southern Region); section K, lot 174, grave 5

Thye, who was raised on a farm and then operated his own farm near Northfield, began his political career as a deputy commissioner of agriculture for Minnesota. He was elected lieutenant governor in 1942 and became governor the following year when *Harold Stassen* resigned to enter military service during World War II. Thye was elected to a full term as governor and then served two terms in the U.S. Senate.

LUTHER YOUNGDAHL
27TH STATE GOVERNOR, 1947–51
May 29, 1896–June 21, 1978
Arlington National Cemetery, Arlington, Virginia

A justice of the Minnesota Supreme Court who was elected to the first of three terms as Minnesota governor in 1946, Youngdahl did not complete his final term as he left office after being appointed a federal district judge in 1951. Youngdahl is one of two Minnesota governors (*Cushman Davis* being the other) buried in Arlington.

C. ELMER ANDERSON
28TH STATE GOVERNOR, 1951–55
March 16, 1912–January 22, 1998
Evergreen Cemetery, Brainerd, Crow Wing County
(North Central/West Region); block 34, lot 21

Not to be confused with Governor *Elmer L. Andersen* (although he often is), Clyde Elmer Anderson had been lieutenant governor under Governor *Harold Stassen* at a time when the two positions were elected separately. While Stassen was elected governor for a third time,

C. Elmer Anderson's grave marker, 2003

in 1942, Anderson was defeated in the lieutenant-governor race by *Edward Thye,* a candidate backed by Stassen. Thus it was Thye, not Anderson, who took over as governor when Stassen resigned to join the Navy in 1943. Anderson was later elected lieutenant governor four more times, which put him into the governor's office when *Luther Youngdahl* resigned in September 1951 to accept a federal judgeship. Anderson was reelected to a second term in 1952, with Elmer L. Andersen chairing his reelection campaign. Anderson later served as mayor of the cities of Nisswa and Brainerd.

ORVILLE FREEMAN
29TH STATE GOVERNOR, 1955–61
May 9, 1918–February 20, 2003
Lakewood Cemetery, Minneapolis, Hennepin County
(Metro Region); section 30, lot 317, grave 1

Freeman was a three-time Minnesota governor who then served as secretary of agriculture under Presidents John F. Kennedy and Lyndon B. Johnson. In the latter role, Freeman was instrumental in the creation of food stamps and other programs designed to create a food safety-net. A second lieutenant in the U.S. Marine Corps during World War II, Freeman was severely wounded while leading a combat patrol in November 1943; hospitalized for eight months, he was awarded the Purple Heart. Following the war, Freeman was an assistant to Minneapolis mayor *Hubert H. Humphrey,* a former partner on the debate team at the University of Minnesota. Freeman and Humphrey were among the key members in the building of the Democratic-Farmer-Labor party.

ELMER L. ANDERSEN
30TH STATE GOVERNOR, 1961–63
June 17, 1909–

(See portrait on page 155.)

KARL F. ROLVAAG
31ST STATE GOVERNOR, 1963–67
July 18, 1913–December 20, 1990

Marker (only) next to Ole E. Rølvaag marker, Oaklawn Cemetery, Northfield, Rice County (Southern Region); section K, lot 85, grave 5

Son of novelist and professor *Ole E. Rølvaag* (who used the traditional Norwegian spelling of his surname), Karl Fritjof Rolvaag served the first four-year governor's term after narrowly defeating incumbent *Elmer L. Andersen* in an election that was not settled by recount until nearly five months later. Rolvaag's cremated ashes were scattered near his father's vacation cabin in Itasca County. *(See portrait on page 135.)*

HAROLD LEVANDER
32ND STATE GOVERNOR, 1967–71
October 10, 1910–March 30, 1992

Acacia Park Cemetery, Mendota Heights, Dakota County (Metro Region); Poplar section, block 7, lot 4, grave 12

Harold LeVander practiced law for more than thirty years before winning the first election he ever entered—for governor of Minnesota in 1966. LeVander created the Metropolitan Council for the Twin Cities area in addition to regional development commissions for the rest of Minnesota while also initiating state aid to local units of government. Under LeVander, the Department of Human Rights and the Pollution Control Agency were created, as well as the state's first sales tax.

WENDELL ANDERSON
33RD STATE GOVERNOR, 1971–76
February 1, 1933–

RUDY PERPICH
34TH STATE GOVERNOR, 1976–79
June 27, 1928–September 21, 1995
Lakewood Cemetery, Minneapolis, Hennepin County
(Metro Region); section 30, lot 385, grave 3

An Iron Range dentist, Perpich moved from the Hibbing School Board to the state legislature to the position of lieutenant governor under *Wendell Anderson*. Anderson resigned in late 1976 to have Perpich, who ascended to the governor's office, appoint Anderson to the U.S. Senate seat vacated by Walter Mondale after he was elected vice president. The maneuvering to put Anderson in the Senate was controversial, and both principals to the appointment lost their elections in 1978. Perpich ran again in 1982 and was elected, becoming the first person to serve non-consecutive terms as Minnesota governor. Perpich was reelected four years later but lost to *Arne Carlson* in a bid for another term in 1990. Perpich died of cancer less than five years later.

AL QUIE
35TH STATE GOVERNOR, 1979–83
September 18, 1923–

RUDY PERPICH
34TH (*see* page 115) AND
36TH STATE GOVERNOR, 1983–91

ARNE CARLSON
37TH STATE GOVERNOR, 1991–99
September 10, 1934–

JESSE VENTURA (BORN JAMES GEORGE JANOS)
38TH STATE GOVERNOR, 1999–2003
July 15, 1951–

TIM PAWLENTY
39TH STATE GOVERNOR, 2003–
November 27, 1960–

THE GREAT BEYOND

RELIGIOUS LEADERS

Although many non-Minnesotans consider it to be populated mostly by Lutheran Norwegian bachelor farmers à la Lake Wobegon, the state has much more religious diversity, as shown by this sampling of spiritual advisors.

JOSEPH CRETIN

December 19, 1799–
February 22, 1857

Calvary Cemetery, St. Paul, Ramsey County (Metro Region); section 7

Joseph Cretin, about 1850

Ordained a priest in 1823 in his native France, Cretin soon afterwards arrived in Dubuque, Iowa, to work there and among the Winnebago for ten years. When St. Paul was chosen in 1850 to be the seat of a new diocese, Cretin became its first bishop. As the population of Minnesota increased during the next decade, Cretin organized many new parishes.

SAMUEL HINMAN

1839–March 24, 1890

St. Cornelia's Episcopal Church, near Morton, Redwood County (Southern Region)

An Episcopal missionary, Hinman arrived at the Lower Sioux Agency intending to start a school and church for the Dakota. Before the church could be completed, it was destroyed in the Dakota War of 1862. Nearly twenty-five years later, Hinman resumed his mission work at the Lower Agency. With twenty acres of land provided by

Andrew Good Thunder, a new church was built. More than one hundred years later, St. Cornelia's Episcopal Church (named after the first wife of Bishop *Henry Whipple,* who had originally sent Hinman to the agency) remains a key part of the Lower Sioux community.

JOHN IRELAND
September 11, 1838–September 25, 1918
**Calvary Cemetery, St. Paul, Ramsey County
(Metro Region); section 7**

Born in Ireland, John Ireland was the first Roman Catholic archbishop of St. Paul. In 1891, three years after becoming archbishop, Ireland devised the controversial Faribault Plan, which allowed the city of Faribault to pay teachers at a parochial school with the provision that the teachers would have no religious observances or teachings during regular school hours. Ireland founded the St. Paul Seminary and donated his private library, said to be one of the most comprehensive in the region, to the seminary.

JOHN KA-KA-GESICK
*May 14, 1844–
December 6, 1968*
**Indian Burial Grounds (formerly
Highland Park Cemetery),
on private property, Warroad,
Roseau County (North
Central/West Region)**

Ka-Ka-Gesick was a Chippewa spiritual leader and trapper reported to have lived for more than 124 years. It is believed that he was at least 110 at the

John Ka-Ka-Gesick gazed at a ceremonial pipe, about 1960

time of his death. While there is a record that puts his year of birth as 1844, the full birth date is not given. In

1964 the Warroad village leaders selected May 14 as his "official" birthday. Ka-Ka-Gesick was buried in traditional Indian burial grounds along the Warroad River on the Ka-Beck-A-Nung Trail. The spirit house over his grave, along with other three houses, remains on the grounds of what is now a private home in Warroad. *(See also Na-Ma-Pock)*

ALBERT MINDA
July 30, 1895–January 15, 1977
Temple Israel Memorial Park, Minneapolis,
Hennepin County (Metro Region); lot 517, grave 4

An author, lecturer, and civic and religious leader, Minda was named One of the Hundred Living Great in 1949 when Minnesota observed its centennial as a territory. Minda led Temple Israel, Minneapolis's oldest and largest Jewish congregation, from 1922 to 1963. He was one of the organizers of the Minneapolis Urban League and chairman of the Citizens League's Public Library Commission. Minda was also a lecturer at Hamline University in St. Paul and author of a number of books, including a history of the temple.

JOHN ROACH
July 31, 1921–July 11, 2003
Resurrection Cemetery, Mendota Heights,
Dakota County (Metro Region); section 1, block 15

Born in Prior Lake and ordained a priest in 1946, Archbishop Roach led the Archdiocese of St. Paul and Minneapolis from 1975 to 1995. His successor, Harry Flynn, called Roach an "outstanding church leader" who "made major contributions to the lives of both Catholics and non-Catholics in this archdiocese. He was instrumental in calling national attention to social justice issues, fostering ecumenism at the local level, and building up the work of the laity." The first Minnesota native to head the archdiocese, Roach was noted for his work in interfaith relations, including the development and signing of the Lutheran-Catholic Covenant. He also served as president of the U.S. Conference of Catholic Bishops from 1980 to 1983.

HENRY WHIPPLE
February 15, 1822–September 16, 1901
Cathedral of Our Merciful Saviour, Faribault, Rice County (Southern Region)

Whipple arrived in Minnesota in the late 1850s and became the first bishop of the Episcopal Diocese of Minnesota. The Cathedral of Our Merciful Saviour in Faribault developed from the efforts of the Reverend James Lloyd Breck, who had persuaded Whipple to base his Episcopal outreach efforts in Faribault and then raised the money for construction of the church. A friend to both the Dakota and the Ojibwe in Minnesota, Whipple worked for the reform of U.S. Indian policies and an Indian mission program. Upon the request for a church and reservation school in 1860, Whipple dispatched *Samuel Hinman* to work with the Dakota at the Lower Sioux Agency. In 1862 Whipple sent a letter to President Lincoln, warning of the dangers of the government's Indian policies, inequities that led to the Dakota War in August and September of that year. Following the conflict, Whipple interceded on behalf of the more than three hundred Dakota who were condemned to death for their part in the war, earning the name "Straight Tongue" from the Dakota for standing up to the prevailing mob attitude. Lincoln approved execution for only thirty-nine of the Dakota, a number ultimately reduced to thirty-eight. Whipple is interred in a crypt within the Faribault cathedral.

REUBEN YOUNGDAHL
May 7, 1911–March 2, 1968
Lakewood Cemetery, Minneapolis, Hennepin County
(Metro Region); section 60, lot 313A, grave 1

Youngdahl was pastor for thirty years at Mount Olivet
Lutheran Church in Minneapolis. During his tenure,
Mount Olivet grew from three hundred to more than
ten thousand members, making it the largest Lutheran
congregation in the country. Youngdahl had been a
basketball star at Gustavus Adolphus College. At his
first pastorate, in Marshalltown, Iowa, in the mid-1930s,
Youngdahl supplanted his income by playing professional basketball. Youngdahl's brother *Luther* was governor of Minnesota from 1947 to 1951.

OUT OF BUSINESS

ENTREPRENEURS

Minnesota has been one of the nation's leaders in business activity. More than just natural resources and raw materials—whether they be wheat, water power, taconite, or forests—it has been the integrity, skill, and daring of the business leaders themselves that have built its business climate in ventures both large and small.

FERRIS ALEXANDER
September 16, 1918–January 31, 2003
Fort Snelling National Cemetery, Minneapolis, Hennepin County (Metro Region); section 19, grave 1184

After serving in the U.S. Army during World War II, Alexander became a well-known magazine and book distributor sometimes called the pornography king of Minnesota as he tested the boundaries of free speech. In 1990 Alexander was convicted of racketeering, obscenity, and tax fraud, and became the first person in the United States to be sentenced to prison for pornography violations under the federal Racketeer Influenced and Corrupt Organizations Act.

A. P. ANDERSON
November 22, 1862–May 7, 1943
Burnside Cemetery, Red Wing, Goodhue County (Southern Region); east end of cemetery

A farmer, educator, scientist, botanist, and poet, Alexander Pierce Anderson is best remembered as the creator of the process for puffing cereal grains discovered when, in 1901, he was able to heat corn starch to a temperature high enough to cause it to explode, thus turning the expanded starch granules into a porous puffed mass.

He started the Anderson Puffed Rice Company and eventually received twenty-five patents for the puffing process and the machinery used to manufacture it.

JEANNE AUERBACHER
December 1, 1898–January 28, 1975
**Temple Israel Memorial Park, Minneapolis,
Hennepin County (Metro Region); lot 623, grave 2**

Auerbacher was a fashion coordinator and manager of the elegant Oval Room at Dayton's department store in downtown Minneapolis for many years.

GEORGE BARNUM
October 10, 1843–August 2, 1936
**Forest Hill Cemetery, Duluth, St. Louis County
(Northeast Region); section L, block C, lot 6**

Barnum arrived in Minnesota in 1867 and eventually became active in the grain business in Duluth. He organized the Barnum Grain Company in 1894 and held the position of president until he died more than forty years later. Barnum became one of the incorporators of the Duluth Board of Trade. A Civil War veteran, who had served in the One Hundredth New York Volunteer Regiment, he participated in the 1862 Peninsular Campaign and is reported to have been present when Robert E. Lee surrendered at Appomattox Court House in Virginia in April 1865.

FRANCIS ATHERTON BEAN
January 16, 1840–February 20, 1930
**Maple Lawn Cemetery, Faribault, Rice County
(Southern Region); section T, lot 6**

Bean was a miller who founded what eventually became International Multifoods. His first business—his father's flour mill in Faribault—went bankrupt. More than twenty years later, when he started a new mill in

New Prague, Bean repaid his creditors, with interest, from the first failed mill. Bean also served on the executive committee of the Boy Scouts of America and was active in local Scouting.

JAMES FORD BELL
August 16, 1879–May 7, 1961
Lakewood Cemetery, Minneapolis, Hennepin County (Metro Region); section 23, lot 10, grave 48

A miller, as well as a pioneer in waterfowl conservation, Bell created General Mills by leading the consolidation of the Washburn Crosby Company with other regional milling companies in 1928. Bell was instrumental in the development of the Museum of Natural History (which was renamed in his honor in 1966) at the University of Minnesota, where he was a regent from 1939 until his death in 1961. Bell also established the American Wildlife Foundation (now the Delta Waterfowl Foundation), an organization devoted to the needs of waterfowl and wetlands.

MAUD BORUP (MAUD BORUP KOUNTZE)
March 14, 1877–October 16, 1960
Oakland Cemetery, St. Paul, Ramsey County (Metro Region); block 15, lot 4

A St. Paul candymaker since 1907, Maud Borup started making chocolates in her home before opening a factory and store. She founded Maud Borup Chocolates and sold her candy throughout the world. Her customers reportedly included European royalty such as Queen Elizabeth II of England.

Maud Borup, about 1955

ADOLF BREMER
July 24, 1869–October 9, 1939
Calvary Cemetery, St. Paul, Ramsey County
(Metro Region); section 33, block 2

Born in Germany, Bremer arrived in St. Paul at the age of seventeen, became associated with the *Jacob Schmidt* Brewing Company in 1888, and eight years later married the founder's daughter. He became the company's vice president in 1901 and eventually its president. Bremer and his brother, Otto, had experience in banking in their native land, and Adolf was a financier, holding stock in his brother's expanding bank holdings in the Northwest. Both Bremers were active in the Democratic party and were friends with President Franklin Roosevelt. Adolf Bremer was the father of Edward Bremer, a banker who was kidnapped and later released by the Ma Barker-Alvin Karpis gang in St. Paul in 1934.

ARCHIBALD BUSH
March 5, 1887–January 16, 1966
Oakland Cemetery, St. Paul, Ramsey County
(Metro Region); block 69, lot 2

Bush had a long career in sales and management at Minnesota Mining and Manufacturing (3M) and served as chairman of the company's executive committee, amassing a fortune through purchases of 3M stock. In 1953, Bush and his wife, Edyth, an actress and dancer who left the stage to marry him, started the Bush Foundation, the second-largest private foundation in Minnesota, to encourage and promote charitable, scientific, literary, and educational efforts.

CURT CARLSON
July 9, 1914–February 19, 1999
**Lakewood Cemetery, Minneapolis, Hennepin County
(Metro Region); section 23, lot 125, grave 30**

With a net worth of nearly $1.7 billion, Carlson was
ranked as the richest Minnesotan in 1998 by *Forbes*
magazine. Carlson had started the Gold Bond Stamp
Company in 1938 with a $55 loan, building the
trading-stamp company into a multi-billion dollar
travel, marketing, and hospitality empire.

CHESTER A. CONGDON
June 12, 1853–November 21, 1916
**Forest Hill Cemetery, Duluth, St. Louis County
(Northeast Region); section I, block 4, lot 1**

A Duluth mining magnate and progressive politician,
Chester Adgate Congdon was one of the state's leading
citizens and possibly Minnesota's wealthiest man at the
time of his death. A native of New York, Congdon arrived in Minnesota in 1880 and began a law practice in
St. Paul. He served as an assistant U.S. attorney from
1881 to 1886. In 1892 Congdon moved to Duluth and
entered the mining business. He was president of a
number of companies, legal counsel for another, and
one of the foremost developers of mining property.
Congdon served in the Minnesota legislature and was a
member of the Republican national committee. In the
early 1900s Congdon built Glensheen, a magnificent
mansion on Lake Superior that received great notoriety
in 1977 when Congdon's daughter, *Elisabeth Congdon*,
and her night nurse, *Velma Pietila*, were murdered there.

DON DANNHEIM
May 12, 1913–August 21, 1999
**St. Paul's Evangelical Lutheran Church Cemetery, New Ulm,
Brown County (Southern Region); block 10E, lot 33**

Owner of the New Ulm Dairy, which he inherited from

his father, "Big Don" Dannheim was known for a marketing ability that drew people from neighboring states to buy his milk. He was a supporter of New Ulm businesses, helping to develop the city's downtown district, and also an active member of Toastmasters International, frequently supplying free ice cream for the organization's social events.

WILLIAM DUNWOODY
March 14, 1841–February 8, 1914
Lakewood Cemetery, Minneapolis, Hennepin County (Metro Region); section 10, lot 82, grave 3.5

A Minneapolis financier and merchant miller, Dunwoody left nearly three million dollars in his will to establish Dunwoody Institute, which has been recognized as an "Institute of Excellence" by the National Center of Research in Vocational Education.

GUILLERMO FRIAS
October 2, 1929–February 21, 2004
Resurrection Cemetery, Mendota Heights, Dakota County (Metro Region); Chapel Mausoleum, elevation D, tier G, niche 18

Born in Mexico, Frias came to the United States in the 1940s and in 1953 moved to St. Paul, where he transformed a former rug-cleaning shop into the Boca Chica Restaurante, a landmark on the city's West Side.

DEIL GUSTAFSON
May 5, 1931–April 2, 1999
Zion Cemetery, Hampton Township, Dakota County, (Metro Region)

A real estate magnate, Gustafson owned Summit Banks in the Twin Cities and the Tropicana, a Las Vegas casino with ties to organized crime. He served time in prison in the 1980s for fraudulent financial dealings involving the Tropicana. Gustafson, who also taught economics at the University of Minnesota, was noted for a huge stuffed bear, which he is said to have bagged on a hunting expedition, displayed in the lobby of his office in the Flour Exchange Building in Minneapolis, an office he shared for a time with former Minneapolis Lakers basketball great George Mikan.

THEODORE HAMM
October 14, 1825–July 31, 1903
Calvary Cemetery, St. Paul, Ramsey County (Metro Region); section 32, block 37

Hamm was the founder of the Theodore Hamm Brewing Company and the grandfather of *William Hamm Jr.*, a 1933 kidnapping victim of the Barker-Karpis gang.

JAMES J. HILL
September 16, 1838–May 29, 1916
Resurrection Cemetery, Mendota Heights, Dakota County (Metro Region); section 15

Known as the "Empire Builder," Hill had holdings in a number of businesses, including mining, shipping, power development, milling, and banking, but he is best known as the railroad baron who developed and expanded the Great Northern Railway north to Canada and across the Rocky Mountains to the Puget Sound. Born in Rockwood, Ontario, Hill arrived in St. Paul in 1856 and worked as a freight-forwarding agent. He started a steamboat line on the Red River between Fort Abercrombie in the Dakota Territory and Fort Garry (now Winnipeg). From 1866 to 1878, Hill was the agent for the St. Paul & Pacific Railroad, which he and his partners purchased. He reorganized the railroad into the St. Paul, Minneapolis & Manitoba, which eventually became a part of the Great Northern Railway Company that he created as part of his mission to reach the Pacific Northwest. Hill amassed great wealth and built a magnificent red sandstone home on Summit Avenue in

St. Paul. His legacy in Minneapolis is the curved Stone Arch Bridge that spans the Mississippi River downstream from St. Anthony Falls.

GEORGE A. HORMEL
December 4, 1860–June 6, 1946
Oakwood Cemetery, Austin, Mower County (Southern Region); in section between Center & Sunset Sts. and between Harmony Ave. & Chapel Dr.

While vacationing in Austin in 1887, George Hormel learned of a butcher shop that had closed because of a fire. Hormel purchased and reopened the shop, thus propelling himself on his way to becoming a meat-packing magnate, the head of a company that bears his name and became famous for its canned chili and beef stew as well as Spam, a product that now has its own museum in Austin.

WALTER C. JAMES (KIM WAH)
February 6, 1891–February 3, 1971
Lakewood Cemetery, Minneapolis, Hennepin County (Metro Region); Mausoleum, room 207, tier 0-1, crypt A2

Kim Wah, also known as Walter C. James, was a Chinese American leader in the Twin Cities. Born in Yakima, Washington, James arrived in Midwest in the early-twentieth century. In Minneapolis he opened the Canton Grill in the Dyckman Hotel and later established the Nankin Cafe. James served as a liaison between Chinese immigrants and other Minneso-

Walter C. James (Kim Wah), 1940

tans and converted one of the floors of the Nankin into clubrooms for immigrants.

FRANCIS JOHNSON
April 17, 1904–October 24, 1989

Dassel Community Cemetery, Dassel, Meeker County (Southern Region); block 3, section 2, lot 298. grave 1 1/2

Son of U.S. Senator *Magnus Johnson,* Francis Johnson was the creator of the world's largest ball of twine made by one person. This masterpiece is displayed in Darwin, where Twine Ball Days has become an annual celebration. Johnson started the ball in 1950 and often spent several hours a day in wrapping; the ball eventually reached twelve feet in diameter and required the use of railroad jacks to keep its growth circular as he added to its girth.

FREDERICK M. JONES
May 17, 1893–February 21, 1961

Fort Snelling National Cemetery, Minneapolis, Hennepin County (Metro Region); section D, grave 2802

An African American inventor, Jones took the skills that he had developed while a teenager as a mechanic to register more than sixty patents during his career, which also included many inventions that were not patented. His first patent, in 1939, was for a movie-house apparatus that delivered tickets and returned change. Jones specialized in air-conditioning and refrigeration equipment and cofounded the U.S. Thermo Control Company (now Thermo King). He also invented x-ray and audio equipment.

ROY KUEHMICHEL
August 12, 1898–November 26, 1951

Evergreen Cemetery, Brainerd, Crow Wing County (North Central/West Region); block 11, lot 47

Kuehmichel was a longtime businessman and civic booster in Brainerd and, along with a partner, purchased a giant Paul Bunyan statue and brought it to Brainerd, where it held court at Paul Bunyan Land, an amusement park that closed in 2003. Kuehmichel was president of the Brainerd-Baxter Corporation, which owned Paul Bunyan Land.

THOMAS LOWRY
February 27, 1843–February 4, 1909
Lakewood Cemetery, Minneapolis, Hennepin County (Metro Region); section 27, lot 1

An attorney turned financier and real-estate developer in Minneapolis, Lowry saw the need for public transportation and became responsible for the development of the Twin City Rapid Transit Company in the late-nineteenth century. Also a business and civic leader and a member of Minneapolis society, Lowry along with his wife, Beatrice, lived in a grand mansion atop Hennepin Hill (now Lowry Hill) on Groveland Terrace, a property later purchased by T. B. Walker, who built the Walker Art Center at the base of the hill.

FRANKLIN C. MARS
September 24, 1883–April 8, 1934
Lakewood Cemetery, Minneapolis, Hennepin County (Metro Region); section 31, lot 6

Born in Newport, Minnesota, Mars returned to his home state after ten years in Washington and began his own company, manufacturing candy bars. Mars's business took off with the creation of the Milky Way bar in 1923, and his name has become synonymous with candy.

LEONIDAS MERRITT
February 20, 1844–May 9, 1926
**Oneota Cemetery, Duluth, St. Louis County
(Northeast Region); section H, block 7, lot 5, grave 3**

A Duluth civic leader who established and lost a fortune, then built a new one, Merritt is credited with the discovery of the first iron ore on the Mesabi Range in northeastern Minnesota in 1890. Merritt and his brothers formed the "Seven Iron Men," who made great contributions to the growth of the mining industry in the region after following the advice of their father, who had found ore samples more than twenty years before, to explore the area. The Merritts also created a railroad to transport their product and materials. The first train of ore from the Mesabi Range to the Merritts' newly built dock at Duluth arrived on July 22, 1893, just in time for the panic of 1893. Heavy building expenses eventually drove the Merritts into the hands of John D. Rockefeller, who bought enough shares to eventually take control of the enterprise. Merritt lost most of his money, but he acquired additional mining rights and regained some of his wealth.

MINA PETERSON
December 18, 1890–March 5, 1996
**Winthrop Cemetery, Winthrop, Sibley County
(Southern Region); section A, lot 4, block 32**

Known as the "Pie Lady of Winthrop," Peterson was a fixture at Lyle's Cafe in Winthrop, achieving notoriety for her prodigious production of pies. She worked until she was in her nineties and, by her own count, baked more than eighty thousand pies.

ELIZABETH QUINLAN
February 15, 1863–September 15, 1947
**St. Mary's Cemetery, Minneapolis, Hennepin County
(Metro Region); section 10, block 11, lot 3, grave 7**

Quinlan was one of the first female merchandising executives in the United States. She was the cofounder, with Fred Young, of Minneapolis's Young-Quinlan department store in 1894 and served as its president until 1945.

TIGER JACK ROSENBLOOM
April 10, 1907–August 5, 2001
Elmhurst Cemetery, St. Paul, Ramsey County (Metro Region); block 51, lot 1011

Operating out of a shed at 369 North Dale Street on the north side of the Interstate 94 highway at the corner of Dale and St. Anthony Avenue since 1949, Rosenbloom became one of St. Paul's best-known and most beloved businessmen. His small store remained as the city's African American Rondo neighborhood around it was largely destroyed by highway construction in the 1960s. Rosenbloom earned

Tiger Jack Rosenbloom in front of his store, greeting passersby, 1989

the name "Tiger Jack" as a boxer in the 1920s and 1930s. In 2003 a one-block portion of Dale was renamed Mr. and Mrs. Tiger Jack Street in honor of Rosenbloom and his wife, Nurceal. After the shed was removed from its site, Mrs. Rosenbloom donated it to the Minnesota Historical Society.

PERCY ROSS
November 22, 1916–November 10, 2001
**Adath-Yeshurun Cemetery, Edina, Hennepin County
(Metro Region); section 8, block 1, lot 1, grave 16**

Ross was a Twin Cities philanthropist who flaunted his
wealth and found showy ways of giving his money
away, including hurling silver dollars into crowds as he
rode in a parade. Ross grew up on the Upper Peninsula
of Michigan and moved to Minnesota in 1936. By the
end of the 1960s he had become a multi-millionaire
and used his money to achieve celebrity status in the
next decade.

TED ROWELL
July 15, 1905–September 25, 1979
**Elm Park Cemetery, Baudette, Lake of the
Woods County (North Central/West Region)**

Rowell was the founder and chairman of the board of
Rowell Laboratories, Inc. in Lake of the Woods County
and a civic leader in Baudette. Rowell, who served as
Baudette mayor for six years during the 1940s, was
largely responsible for the construction of the international bridge in to Ontario. He also owned three certi-
fied tree farms and was once named Minnesota Tree
Farmer of the Year.

JACOB SCHMIDT
October 9, 1846–September 2, 1910
**Calvary Cemetery, St. Paul, Ramsey County
(Metro Region); section 33, block 2**

Born in Bavaria, Schmidt learned the brewing business in
his native land before arriving in the United States when
he was twenty and working at breweries in New York
and the Midwest, including Schell's in New Ulm, Minnesota, and Hamm's in St. Paul. In 1884 he purchased
a half-interest in a St. Paul brewery that was eventually
incorporated as the Jacob Schmidt Brewing Company.

BOB SHORT

July 20, 1917–November 20, 1982

Resurrection Cemetery, Mendota Heights, Dakota County (Metro Region); section 15, block 16, grave 7

An entrepreneur, political maverick, and sports team owner, Short made his fortune with the first and third activities while experiencing, and causing, frustration with the second. He acquired his first significant wealth by taking over and expanding a transportation company. From there he went on to purchase hotels and real estate, along the way gaining control of the Minneapolis Lakers, a basketball team that he moved to Los Angeles in 1960 and sold five years later for five million dollars. In 1968 Short purchased baseball's Washington Senators, another team he would uproot and move within a few years. Short was an active member of the Democratic-Farmer-Labor party in Minnesota. Although never elected to office, he defeated Don Fraser for the party's nomination for the U.S. Senate in 1978, an upset that split the DFL and opened the way for Republican candidate Dave Durenberger to win the general election.

Bob Short (left) and *Karl F. Rolvaag* engaged in primary-election activity at the Minnesota State Fair, 1966

ROSE TOTINO
January 16, 1915–June 21, 1994
Sunset Memorial Park, Minneapolis, Hennepin County (Metro Region); block 14, section 135, grave 16

Having tasted the baked pies while visiting relatives in Pennsylvania, Totino began making pizzas for friends and from that simple beginning started a business in a small northeast Minneapolis kitchen with her husband, Jim, in 1951. Ten years later the Totinos launched a line of frozen pizzas and eventually sold their enterprise to the Pillsbury Company for twenty million dollars. The Totinos donated money to Northwestern College in Roseville and to Grace High School (renamed Totino-Grace High School in their honor) in Fridley.

BRUCE WATSON
December 1, 1932–March 18, 2004
Fort Snelling National Cemetery, Minneapolis, Hennepin County (Metro Region); section 18, grave 433

A pioneer of forensic meteorology, Watson was reported to have the largest private collection of water data in Minnesota. Taking records from a weather station in his backyard, Watson operated his own company, providing long-range forecasts and serving as a consultant. A popular public speaker, Watson was to have made a presentation on "Weather: A Story of Whirlpools" to an American Water Works Association shortly before his death.

REIKO WESTON
September 27, 1928–May 7, 1988
Lakewood Cemetery, Minneapolis, Hennepin County (Metro Region); section 36, lot 8E, grave 6

Weston came to the United States in 1952 with her husband, Norman, whom she met while working in Douglas MacArthur's headquarters in Tokyo following

World War II. In 1959, Weston opened Fuji-Ya, the first Japanese restaurant in Minneapolis. Two years later, she moved Fuji-Ya on top of the ruins of a burned-out flour mill on the west bank of the Mississippi River, and the restaurant became the first major development in the riverfront's renaissance. Weston was inducted into the Minnesota Business Hall of Fame in 1980 and was named Minnesota Businesswoman of the Year in 1987.

HOWARD WONG
September 11, 1912–September 19, 1993
Resurrection Cemetery, Mendota Heights, Dakota County (Metro Region); section 62, block 14, lot 2, grave 1

Born in Canton, China, Wong opened a restaurant named after himself in Bloomington in 1966. Howard Wong's was noted for its Cantonese cuisine as well as for the large metal sculpture by Minnesota artist Donald Danielson of a fire-breathing dragon, located in front of the restaurant. (The sculpture was later moved to Minnesota State University Moorhead, which uses a dragon as a school symbol.) Wong had been president of the state restaurant associations of Minnesota and South Dakota. He was friends with baseball manager Billy Martin and was with Martin in 1979 at a Bloomington hotel when Martin beat up marshmallow-salesman Joseph Cooper in a highly publicized incident that caused Martin to be fired from the New York Yankees five days later.

POST SEASON

SPORTS NOTABLES

Scattered throughout Minnesota are the graves of members of various sports halls of fame and many other fine athletes. There is, as yet, no grave for a member of the Baseball Hall of Fame. For many years, the only Minnesota-born player in the Hall of Fame was Charles "Chief" Bender, who was born in Crow Wing County and lived on the White Earth Indian Reservation until he was sent at a very young age to Philadelphia for his education. Bender is buried just north of Philadelphia, where he achieved fame as a star pitcher for Connie Mack's Philadelphia Athletics in the early-twentieth century.

LOU BARLE
June 23, 1916–December 30, 1996
Lakeview Cemetery, Coleraine, Itasca County (Northeast Region); block 2, new addition, lot 27, west half

Brothers Lou and Frank Barle were stars on the Gilbert High School basketball teams in the early 1930s, with Lou going on to an outstanding collegiate career in football, basketball, and track at Duluth State Teachers College (now the University of Minnesota Duluth). Lou played in the National Football League briefly with the Detroit Lions in 1938 and the Cleveland Rams in 1939. During that period he also played for the Oshkosh All-Stars in the National Basketball League and was a starting forward on the Oshkosh team that won the NBL championship in 1941. Barle later coached a variety of sports at Sauk Centre and, upon his return to the Mesabi Iron Range, at Greenway High School in Coleraine.

BERT BASTON
December 3, 1894–November 15, 1979
Lakewood Cemetery, Minneapolis, Hennepin County
(Metro Region); section 8, lot 386, grave 6

Baston was the first two-time All-America football selection for the Minnesota Gophers, in 1915 and 1916. Although the forward pass had been rarely used up to that time, he achieved fame as a receiver, teaming with Pudge Wyman to give the Gophers their first real passing combination. Baston was inducted into the College Football Hall of Fame in 1954.

BERNIE BIERMAN
March 11, 1894–
March 7, 1977
Sunset Memorial Park,
Minneapolis, Hennepin County
(Metro Region); block 7D,
section 102, space 1

Bernie Bierman, about 1915

Known as the "Grey Eagle,"
Bierman was the coach of
the Minnesota Gophers football team before and after
World War II, leading the
Gophers to five national
championships. Bierman
competed in football, basketball, baseball, and track at
Litchfield High School before enrolling at Minnesota.
He captained the 1915 Gophers football team, which
shared the Big Ten title with Illinois, the last title Minnesota won until Bierman returned to the school as
coach in 1932. The Gophers' first national title under
Bierman came in 1934 when they were undefeated and
outscored their opponents, 270 to 38. The team won
the championship the next two years and then again in
1940 and 1941. Bierman was inducted into the College
Football Hall of Fame in 1955.

MACEO BREEDLOVE
August 7, 1900–May 12, 1993
**Crystal Lake Cemetery, Minneapolis, Hennepin County
(Metro Region); section 4/5, lot 212, space 4**

Maceo Breedlove was an outstanding hitter on a number of independent black baseball teams in the 1920s and 1930s, including the Twin Cities Colored Giants. In 1935 the Giants played a series of games against an integrated semi-pro team in Bismarck, North Dakota, that had future Hall of Fame pitchers Hilton Smith and Satchel Paige. On August 10, Breedlove hit a home run off Smith, and the next day he had two doubles and two home runs against Paige. Breedlove later was a popular vendor at Minnesota Twins games in Metropolitan Stadium.

FRANK BRIMSEK
September 26, 1913–November 11, 1993
**Calvary Cemetery, Virginia, St. Louis County
(Northeast Region); section 28**

Brimsek is one of only three people (fellow Minnesotans *Francis X. "Moose" Goheen* and *John Mariucci* being the other two) inducted into both the Hockey Hall of Fame in Toronto, Ontario, and the U.S. Hockey Hall of Fame in Eveleth, Minnesota. A goalie from Eveleth, Brimsek earned the name "Mr. Zero" when he produced six shutouts in his first eight games in the National Hockey League. He received both the Calder Trophy as the league's top rookie and the Vezina Trophy as the best goaltender in 1938–39 while helping the Boston Bruins win the Stanley Cup. He played on one more Stanley Cup champion team and won one more Vezina Trophy.

HERB BROOKS

August 5, 1937–August 11, 2003

**Roselawn Cemetery, Roseville, Ramsey County
(Metro Region); division 6A, lot 141, grave 7**

Brooks was the coach of the U.S. hockey team that upset the Soviet Union en route to a gold medal in the 1980 Winter Olympics. He had come to the national team from the University of Minnesota, where he had coached the Gophers to three national championships. Brooks later coached in the National Hockey League for the New York Rangers, Minnesota North Stars, New Jersey Devils, and Pittsburgh Penguins and was inducted into the U.S. Hockey Hall of Fame in 1990. He died in a one-car accident on Interstate 35 in Forest Lake.

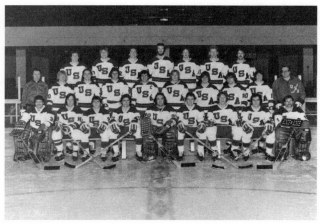

Herb Brooks (second row, far left) and his Miracle on Ice team, 1980

WILLIAM CADREAU ("CHIEF CHOUNEAU")

September 2, 1888–September 17, 1946

**Holy Family Cemeteries, Fond du Lac Indian Reservation,
west of Cloquet, Carlton County (Northeast Region)**

Cadreau grew up playing baseball on the Fond du Lac reservation and played professional baseball for several years. He made one appearance in the major leagues, pitching for the Chicago White Sox on the final day of the 1910 season under the name Chief Chouneau. Although he gave up only two runs in five-and-a-third innings, he was the losing pitcher in the game. Cadreau is buried close to his ancestor Chief *Joseph Naganub.*

PAUL HENRY "LEFTY" CASTNER
February 16, 1897–March 3, 1986
Calvary Cemetery, St. Paul, Ramsey County (Metro Region); section 9, block 1, lot 1, grave 8 (unmarked grave)

Castner was a fullback for Notre Dame under Knute Rockne from 1919 to 1922. His senior season was the first that the Four Horsemen of Don Miller, Elmer Layden, Harry Stuhldreher, and Jim Crowley played together in the same backfield. Castner was also an outstanding hockey and baseball player. In 1923 he pitched six games for the Chicago White Sox.

LOUIS COOKE
February 15, 1868–August 19, 1943
Lakewood Cemetery, Minneapolis, Hennepin County (Metro Region); section 25, lot 366, grave 5

Cooke received his medical degree from the University of Vermont and a two-year degree in physical education from the Young Men's Christian Association International Training School in Springfield, Massachusetts. It was his YMCA work that brought "Doc" Cooke to Minnesota in 1896. While briefly maintaining his position as physical director of the Minneapolis YMCA, Cooke joined the University of Minnesota staff and organized the university's physical education department and intercollegiate athletics program. Cooke coached a variety of sports for the Gophers, although he was most noted for his twenty-seven seasons as head coach of the basketball team, which won two Helms Athletic Foundation national championships. Cooke also collaborated with equipment manager Oscar Munson in inaugurating the

tradition of the Little Brown Jug, the football trophy
traveling between the Gophers and Michigan Wolver-
ines. "If you want it, you'll have to win it," is reported
as Cooke's response to Michigan's request for the return
of its water jug, which Michigan forgot after its 1903
game at Minnesota.

MARY BENDER COOLEY
May 5, 1857–July 16, 1930
Wildwood Cemetery, Norris Township, Lake of the
Woods County (North Central/West Region)

Cooley was the mother of Charles "Chief" Bender (*see*
page 138), the first Minnesota-born player in the Baseball Hall of Fame. While Bender grew up in Pennsylvania, Cooley remained in Minnesota until she died in a
car accident.

KER DUNLOP
August 16, 1859–May 26, 1939
Oakland Cemetery, St. Paul, Ramsey County
(Metro Region); block 103, lot 55

Called the "Dean of Northwest Curlers," Dunlop was one
of the few residents of the United States to be honored
with a life membership in the Manitoba Curling Club.
A native of Scotland, Dunlop moved to St. Paul in 1898
and was a loyal fan of the St. Paul Saints baseball team
and, by his own admission, attended more than three
thousand Saints games.

AMBROSE "LEFTY" EBNET
December 8, 1911–April 1, 1980
St. Mary's Cemetery, Holdingford, Stearns County
(North Central/West Region)

Owner of a meat market in Holdingford, Ebnet was better remembered for his long career in amateur baseball.
He is a member of the Minnesota Amateur Baseball

Hall of Fame. Ebnet also pitched professionally for four seasons, with Winnipeg in the Northern League, winning nineteen games in 1935. In 1948 he was part of an all-Ebnet team, formed with his eight brothers and a number of cousins, that played several games against local teams. Lefty was a cousin of *Linus "Skeets" Ebnet,* who died in 1938 after being beaned during a baseball game.

GEORGE "SHOWBOAT" FISHER
January 16, 1899–May 15, 1994
St. Benedict Parish Cemetery, Avon, Stearns County (North Central/West Region)

Fisher acquired the nickname "Showboat" as an outfielder for the St. Louis Cardinals in 1930 when the musical by that name was a hit. Fisher played ninety-two games and hit eight home runs, helping the Cardinals win the National League pennant that year. Raised in St. Anna, Fisher played for the Minneapolis Millers on two different occasions in the 1920s as well as for the Washington Senators in the American League.

"PHANTOM" MIKE GIBBONS & TOMMY GIBBONS
"Phantom" Mike Gibbons, July 20, 1887–August 31, 1956
Tommy Gibbons, March 22, 1891–November 19, 1960
Calvary Cemetery, St. Paul, Ramsey County (Metro Region); Mike: section 40, block 41, lot 2, Tommy: section 49, block 12, lot 15

The Gibbons brothers were boxers from St. Paul's East Side. Both are members of the International Boxing Hall of Fame.

Mike was a middleweight, considered to be one of the best ever in his class even though he never held the championship. Astonishingly fast with his hands and feet, he was known as the "Phantom of St. Paul." Mike was so fast that an opponent, Harry Greb, once shouted to his manager, "From now on, match me with one guy at a time."

Tommy was a heavyweight who fought Jack Dempsey for the world's championship (losing a fifteen-round decision in 1923 in Shelby, Montana). He later served as Ramsey County sheriff for twenty-three years. In the ring Gibbons had eighty-six professional bouts and reportedly was never knocked off his feet.

"Phantom" Mike Gibbons, about 1920

PAUL GIEL
September 29, 1932–May 22, 2002
Lakewood Cemetery, Minneapolis, Hennepin County (Metro Region); section 31, lot 5, grave 25

Giel was an outstanding athlete from Winona who achieved All-America status in baseball and football for the Minnesota Gophers and was runner-up in the voting for the Heisman award in 1953. He pursued baseball professionally and was signed by the New York Giants for a bonus reported to be sixty thousand dollars. After retiring as a player in 1961, Giel worked briefly for the Minnesota Vikings before becoming sports director at WCCO radio, a job he kept until becoming athletic director at Minnesota in 1972. Giel was inducted into the College Football Hall of Fame in 1975.

WALLY GILBERT
December 19, 1900–September 7, 1958
Sunrise Memorial Park, Hermantown, St. Louis County (Northeast Region); Garden of the Christus, lot 161-D, space 1

A gifted athlete in many sports, Gilbert played in the National Football League with the Duluth Eskimos and in major-league baseball with several teams, including four seasons with the Brooklyn Dodgers. He also played minor-league baseball for the Minneapolis Millers in 1923, before reaching the majors, and with the Duluth

Dukes in 1935 and 1936, several years after his major-league career ended. He was also notable in basketball and curling.

FRANCIS X. "MOOSE" GOHEEN
February 9, 1894–November 13, 1979
St. Mary's of the Lake, White Bear Township, Ramsey County (Metro Region); northeast corner of cemetery

Goheen is a member of both the Hockey Hall of Fame in Canada and the U.S. Hockey Hall of Fame in Eveleth. He made the Hockey Hall in Toronto even though he never played in the National Hockey League. Although his nickname belied his actual size, Goheen was a hard-hitting defensemen who played for the St. Paul Athletic Club team. Except for a period during the World War I when he served in the Army, Goheen played with the Athletic Club team from 1915 through 1932. He was also a member of the silver-medal-winning 1920 U.S. Olympic hockey team. Sportswriter *Halsey Hall* once declared, "Nothing in sports could ever beat the sight of Moose Goheen taking the puck, circling behind his own net, and then taking off down that rink, leaping over sticks along the way."

BILL GOLDSWORTHY
August 24, 1944–March 29, 1996
Lakewood Cemetery, Minneapolis, Hennepin County (Metro Region); section 40, lot 512, grave 1

An original member of the Minnesota North Stars, Goldsworthy was one of the team's most colorful and popular players, particularly known for the "Goldy Shuffle," a leg-raising, fist-pumping celebration he per-formed after scoring a goal. Playing right winger, Goldsworthy had a breakout season in 1969–70, leading the National Hockey League West Division with thirty-six goals. His best season came four years later when he scored forty-eight goals. Following his hockey career,

Goldsworthy battled alcoholism and died of complications from AIDS.

ARCHIBALD "MOONLIGHT" GRAHAM
November 9, 1876–August 25, 1965

**Calvary Cemetery, Rochester, Olmsted County
(Southern Region); section 9, lot 4, grave 1 east**

Immortalized in film for his one brief appearance in a major-league baseball game, Graham was better known as a beloved doctor in the Minnesota Iron Range city of Chisholm. He received his medical degree from the University of Maryland in 1905. A few weeks later, on June 29, "Moonlight" Graham made his only appearance with the New York Giants, playing right field. He

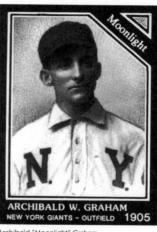

ARCHIBALD W. GRAHAM
NEW YORK GIANTS - OUTFIELD 1905

Archibald "Moonlight" Graham
in his Giants uniform, 1905

did not receive any chances in his two innings in the field nor did he come to bat although he was on deck when the Giants finished batting in the game. It was the extreme brevity of his career that caused author W. P. Kinsella to feature Graham in his book *Shoeless Joe,* which later became the movie *Field of Dreams.* Graham served for more than fifty years as the Chisholm school physician and collaborated on a blood-pressure and heart-test program for children that received national recognition. He is buried with his wife, Alicia, in her hometown of Rochester.

DALLAS HAGEN
March 20, 1947–August 7, 2001
Rosehill Cemetery, Wells, Faribault County (Southern Region); block O, lot 13, grave 5

Hagen was the longtime coach of girls' tennis at Wells High School, where she took four teams to the state tournament. Before arriving in Wells in 1978, Hagen coached girls' tennis at Mahtomedi High School and started the school's gymnastics program. She was inducted into the Athletic Hall of Fame at her alma mater, Augsburg College, and the Minnesota State High School League Hall of Fame.

SPENCER HARRIS
August 12, 1900–July 3, 1982
Lakewood Cemetery, Minneapolis, Hennepin County (Metro Region); section 8, lot 112, grave 6

Duluth native Spencer Harris played ten seasons for the Minneapolis Millers, from 1928 to 1937, hitting better than .300 each year and driving in more than one hundred runs six times. During his first season in Minneapolis, Harris had a .327 batting average and led the American Association in runs, doubles, total bases, home runs, and walks. He also had 127 runs batted in while hitting mainly in the leadoff spot. Harris played professional baseball for twenty-eight years, finally retiring at the age of forty-eight as the minor-league career leader in runs, hits, and doubles.

CURT HENNIG
March 28, 1958–February 10, 2003
Gethsemane Cemetery, New Hope, Hennepin County (Metro Region); Mausoleum, elevation 7, tier F, crypt 30

Hennig was a professional wrestler from Robbinsdale who became known as "Mr. Perfect." Hennig's father, Larry (known as "Pretty Boy" and "The Axe"), had also been a pro wrestler.

PRINCE HONEYCUTT
December 24, 1852–January 29, 1924
Oak Grove Cemetery, Fergus Falls, Otter Tail County
(North Central/West Region); section A, lot 164, grave 5

According to baseball historian Steven Hoffbeck, Honeycutt represents the first recorded instance of an African American baseball player in Minnesota. Honeycutt helped organize the North Star Base Ball Club in Fergus Falls in 1873. During the Civil War, Honeycutt served as a mess boy in the Union army for the unit of Captain James Compton. Following the war, Honeycutt worked for the Compton family in Illinois and accompanied Compton when he moved to Fergus Falls in 1872. In addition to his baseball playing, Honeycutt operated a barbershop in Fergus Falls and also ran for mayor.

JOE HUTTON
June 22, 1899–June 13, 1988
Lakewood Cemetery, Minneapolis, Hennepin County
(Metro Region); Mausoleum, room 115, tier 3, crypt D

Hutton was the basketball coach at Hamline University in St. Paul from 1931 to 1965 and built the Pipers into a small-college power nationally. He compiled a record of 591 wins and 208 losses at Hamline as the team won three National Association of Intercollegiate Basketball championships. As a player, Hutton had been a star at Carleton College in Northfield. He and Carl Nordly led Carleton to three conference titles and two undefeated season with teams that were competitive with much larger schools, including Big Ten teams.

TONY JAROS
February 22, 1920–April 22, 1995
Hillside Memorium Cemetery, Minneapolis, Hennepin County
(Metro Region); section R, 9 feet northwest of lot 209, grave 1

Jaros, who graduated from Edison High School in 1940, is still regarded as one of the greatest multi-sport athletes

Tony Jaros, about 1949

in the history of the Minneapolis City Conference. He played baseball and basketball at the University of Minnesota until he enlisted in the U.S. Army. Following World War II, Jaros signed a contract with the Minneapolis Millers and played three years of professional baseball. He also managed to fit in a pro basketball career in the off-season. Jaros played five years in the Basketball Association of America, National Basketball League, and National Basketball Association with the Chicago Stags and Minneapolis Lakers. He played on three league championship teams with Minneapolis.

HERB JOESTING
April 17, 1905–October 1, 1963
Oakland Cemetery, St. Paul, Ramsey County (Metro Region); block Zion 6, lot 6

A two-time All-America fullback for the Minnesota Gophers, earning the nickname the "Owatonna Thunderbolt," Joesting later coached and played for the Minneapolis Red Jackets in the National Football League. Joesting was inducted into the College Football Hall of Fame in 1954.

WALLY KARBO
August 14, 1915–March 25, 1993
Resurrection Cemetery, Mendota Heights, Dakota County (Metro Region); section 5, block 20, lot 12, grave 1

Karbo was a long time boxing and pro wrestling promoter in Minneapolis who became known for his role as a foil to the bad-guy wrestlers. "There's going to be

fines, there's going to be suspensions" became his trademark refrain in response to the tactics of the villains.
Karbo, along with wrestler Verne Gagne, was the co-
owner of the American Wrestling Association, which
was centered in the Twin Cities.

Wally Karbo refereed a mud-wrestling match, about 1950

MIKE KELLEY
November 2, 1875–June 6, 1955
**Lakewood Cemetery, Minneapolis, Hennepin County
(Metro Region); section 31, lot 246, grave 10**

A Massachusetts native and a major figure in Twin
Cities baseball for many years, Kelley played in the
National League on a Louisville team that included future Hall of Famers Honus Wagner, Rube Waddell, and
Fred Clarke. He was a player-manager on the St. Paul
Saints when the Saints became a charter member of
the American Association in 1902. Kelley worked both
sides of the Mississippi River, serving three separate
stints as manager of the Saints and two with the Minneapolis Millers, and he often had a financial interest
in the team he managed. He was among the last of

the independent owners in the minor leagues, finally selling the Millers in 1946 to the New York Giants after having owned the team since the 1920s. Kelley won more than 2,300 games as manager in the minor leagues, mostly with the Millers and Saints.

VERNAL "BABE" LEVOIR
May 27, 1913–September 7, 1999
Fort Snelling National Cemetery, Minneapolis, Hennepin County (Metro Region); section 9A, grave 55

LeVoir was a great athlete at Marshall High School, in the shadows of the University of Minnesota campus in Minneapolis, who later was a star on the Gophers football teams that were undefeated under *Bernie Bierman* in 1933, 1934, and 1935.

JOHN MARIUCCI
May 18, 1916–March 23, 1987
Fort Snelling National Cemetery, Minneapolis, Hennepin County (Metro Region); section R, grave 1569

Mariucci played hockey and football at Eveleth High School and the University of Minnesota before settling on hockey and entering the professional ranks. He spent five seasons as a defenseman with the Chicago Blackhawks in the 1940s and was twice captain of the team. After retiring as a player, Mariucci became coach of the Minnesota Gophers in 1952. Mariucci made it known he intended to recruit Minnesota players and urged state high schools to develop a hockey program, a challenge that resulted in a rapid increase in teams around the state. When the Minnesota North Stars were formed in 1967, Mariucci left the Gophers to become assistant general manager. Mariucci became a charter member of the U.S. Hockey Hall of Fame in Eveleth in 1973. In 1985 he was inducted, as a builder, into the Hockey Hall of Fame in Canada for his contributions to the growth of amateur and professional hockey in Minnesota. Mariucci Arena, used by the men's hockey team at the university, is named after him.

BOBBY MARSHALL
March 12, 1880–August 27, 1958
Lakewood Cemetery, Minneapolis, Hennepin County (Metro Region); section 15, lot 423, grave 1

Marshall was a multi-sport athlete for the Minnesota Gophers who became the first black to play football in the Big 9 (now Big 10) conference, in 1903. Marshall's long field goal provided the winning margin in the Gophers' victory over Chicago in 1906 to re-establish Minnesota as the unofficial "Champions of the West." He later played in the National Football League even though he was more than forty years old. Marshall was also an outstanding baseball player and played professionally with the St. Paul Colored Gophers. In the first game of a 1909 series between St. Paul and the Chicago Leland Giants, Marshall came to bat for the Colored Gophers with two runners on base in the last of the eleventh inning and his team down by a run. Marshall hit a drive over the fence to score the runners for a 10–9 win. (Marshall's run, under rules of the time, did not count.) Marshall was inducted into the College Football Hall of Fame in 1971.

University of Minnesota football team of 1903, including Bobby Marshall (second row from top, fourth from left)

JOHN MCGOVERN
September 15, 1886–December 14, 1963
**St. Mary's Catholic Cemetery, Arlington,
Sibley County (Southern Region)**

A quarterback and drop-kicker for the Minnesota Gophers, McGovern led the team to the conference championship in 1909 and was named to Walter Camp's All-America team. McGovern was later the sports editor at the *Minneapolis Journal*. He was inducted into the College Football Hall of Fame in 1966.

JIM MITCHELL
1944–March 16, 2004
**Crystal Lake Cemetery, Minneapolis, Hennepin County
(Metro Region); section 27, lot 196, space 5**

A tenor drummer/bass drummer in the University of Minnesota's marching band, Mitchell became the university's first black drum major in 1966, serving until 1970. He later coached drum majors at the university and through 2003 also sang the national anthem before Gophers football games, even after losing both legs to diabetes. As another student wrote of Mitchell, "Jim is the essence of the Minnesota Marching Band. *Jim is the band.*"

BRONKO NAGURSKI
November 3, 1908–January 7, 1990
**St. Thomas Cemetery, International Falls, Koochiching County
(Northeast Region); block G, lot 137**

A bruising, hard-hitting football player on offense and defense (who later brought those same qualities to the ring as a professional wrestler), Nagurski became a larger-than-life figure in the formative years of professional football, playing for the Chicago Bears in the 1930s. Born in Rainy River, Ontario, Nagurski grew up in International Falls. At the University of Minnesota in

1929, Nagurski was named All-America at fullback on offense and tackle on defense. He is a member of the College Football Hall of Fame (inducted in 1951) and became a charter member of the Pro Football Hall of Fame in 1963.

Bronko Nagurski (left) with gubernatorial candidate *Elmer L. Andersen* at Nagurski's service station in International Falls, 1960

JOHN NETT
April 24, 1920–
January 25, 1999
St. Mary's Cemetery, Winona, Winona County (Southern Region); block A, lot 49, grave 12

Nett was the boys' basketball coach at Cotter High School in Winona for more than thirty years and held the record for the most wins by a Minnesota high school basketball coach when he retired in 1983. Cotter won two Class A high school titles, in 1977 and 1982, under Nett, who also coached football and baseball at the school.

MICHAEL O'DOWD
April 5, 1895–July 28, 1957
Calvary Cemetery, St. Paul, Ramsey County (Metro Region); section 49, block 3, lot 21

O'Dowd held the world's middleweight boxing title from 1917 to 1920. He began boxing in Hudson, Wisconsin, during a period when boxing was banned in Minnesota. O'Dowd, who was also a very good baseball player, had 119 fights in a pro career that extended from 1913 to 1922. He was the first American boxing champion to enlist in World War I. Although the two never fought a championship bout, O'Dowd and *"Phantom" Mike Gibbons,* another St. Paul middleweight, had a series of classic fights against one another that are perhaps more famous than those in which O'Dowd fought for or to defend the title.

MARTY O'NEILL
February 18, 1908–February 7, 1983
Resurrection Cemetery, Mendota Heights, Dakota County (Metro Region); section 61, block 27, lot 4, grave 1

Perhaps best remembered as an announcer for All-Star Wrestling in the Twin Cities, O'Neill had an extensive background in sports broadcasting following his playing career. He began broadcasting sports on WMIN radio in 1939 and became the play-by-play announcer for the St. Paul Saints baseball and hockey teams. O'Neill had been an outstanding all-around athlete at Central High School in St. Paul and then played baseball for a variety of amateur teams, several of which won the Minnesota state championship, including the St. Paul Commission Row team in 1936 and Fairfax in 1942. He also played one season of professional baseball, for Duluth in the Northern League in 1934. O'Neill started promoting and announcing professional wrestling in the 1950s. He was elected as a charter member of the Minnesota Amateur Baseball Hall of Fame in 1963.

PAUL OTIS
December 24, 1889–December 15, 1990
Forest Hill Cemetery, Duluth, St. Louis County (Northeast Region); section M, block 11, lot 8

An insurance agent in Duluth, Otis had played four games as an outfielder for the New York Highlanders (later the Yankees) in 1912. At the time of his death, at the age of one hundred years, Otis was the oldest living ex-major-league baseball player.

JULIUS PERLT
September 4, 1903–June 16, 1991
**Sunset Memorial Park, Minneapolis, Hennepin County
(Metro Region); Community Mausoleum, ground level,
corridor 1, section 5, tier A**

Perlt's distinctive voice was a familiar one to sports fans
at Memorial Stadium and Williams Arena as he did the
public-address announcing for Minnesota Gophers
football and basketball for fifty years. Perlt worked for
the convention bureaus in both St. Paul and Minnesota.
In St. Paul he helped to start the state high school
hockey tournament, which was first played at the St.
Paul Auditorium in 1945.

DICK PUTZ
July 20, 1929–September 29, 1990
**Assumption Cemetery, St. Cloud, Stearns County
(North Central/West Region); mausoleum building 7,
west side, row 1, crypt G**

Putz devoted much of his life to amateur baseball and
other sports in the St. Cloud area. He helped to organize Little League teams, served in a variety of positions
with the Central Minnesota Umpires Association, started
the Parochial Athletic Association, and twice served as
the chairman of the Minnesota State Amateur Baseball
tournament. He was elected to the Minnesota Amateur
Baseball Hall of Fame in 1977 and is also a member of
the St. Cloud State University Sports Hall of Fame. Dick
Putz Field in St. Cloud is named after him.

FRANK RABBIT
June 9, 1912–November 3, 1994
**Inger Cemetery, Inger, Leech Lake Indian Reservation,
Itasca County (Northeast Region)**

Rabbit, an Ojibwe, grew up playing baseball wherever
he could around his home on the Leech Lake Indian

Reservation. In the early 1940s Rabbit organized the Inger Indians, a team that won numerous league championships and was known for its outstanding sportsmanship as Rabbit, who was also one of the Indians' top hitters, would not allow abuse of the umpires by any of his players. Rabbit was inducted into the Minnesota Amateur Baseball Hall of Fame in 1965.

ROCKY RACETTE
July 25, 1959–October 17, 1981
Lakewood Cemetery, Minneapolis, Hennepin County (Metro Region); section 8, lot 201, grave 1

Rochelle "Rocky" Racette was a track star at the University of Minnesota who was also the school's homecoming queen in 1980. Racette had just taken her entrance examination for graduate school and was on her way to a geology field trip in Jay Cooke State Park when she was killed in a two-car accident between Willow River and Moose Lake.

ELDON JOHN "RIP" REPULSKI
October 4, 1927–February 10, 1993
Trinity Lutheran Church Cemetery, Sauk Rapids, Benton County (North Central/West Region); section B, lot 16 south, grave 1

Repulski was an all-state athlete from Sauk Rapids who signed a professional baseball contract after graduating from high school in 1947. He made it to the majors in 1953 and was the Cardinals' regular center fielder, playing in 153 games and hitting .275 with 15 home runs. Repulski also played for the Philadelphia Phillies, Los Angeles Dodgers, and Boston Red Sox and hit 106 home runs in his nine-year major-league career.

LARRY ROSENTHAL
May 21, 1910–March 4, 1992

Resurrection Cemetery, Mendota Heights, Dakota County (Metro Region); section 5, block 44, lot 2, grave 2

Larry Rosenthal rose from the sandlots of St. Paul to play professionally for the hometown Saints and eventually in the major leagues. Rosenthal was an outfielder for the Chicago White Sox and several other teams during his eight seasons in the majors.

Larry Rosenthal in Chicago White Sox uniform, 1939

LARRY ROSS
April 12, 1922–May 1, 1995

St. Thomas Cemetery, International Falls, Koochiching County (Northeast Region); block 3, lot 109

Ross was a two-time All-America goalie for the Minnesota Gophers in the early 1950s who achieved even greater fame as coach of the International Falls high school team, which won six state championships under him. He was elected to the U.S. Hockey Hall of Fame in Eveleth in 1988.

EMIL SCHEID
June 13, 1905–July 3, 1982

Calvary Cemetery, Austin, Mower County (Southern Region); section 1-A, lot 45

A plumbing contractor in Austin and the longtime manager of the Austin Packers semi-professional baseball team in the Southern Minnesota League, Scheid employed many players in his plumbing and heating business. One of the best was Bill "Moose" Skowron, who arrived in Austin to play for Scheid following his freshman season at Purdue University. Skowron planned to return to Purdue but played so well for the Packers that he was signed to a pro contract by the New York Yankees. Scheid is a member of the Minnesota Amateur Baseball Hall of Fame.

DICK SIEBERT
February 19, 1912–December 9, 1978
Lakewood Cemetery, Minneapolis, Hennepin County (Metro Region); section 60, lot 816, grave 3

A native of St. Paul who played major-league baseball with the Philadelphia Athletics and St. Louis Cardinals, Siebert came back to Minnesota and coached the Gophers baseball team from 1948 through 1978, leading the team to national championships in 1956, 1960, and 1964 as well as eleven Big Ten titles. Siebert won more than 750 games in his coaching career and was the recipient of the Lefty Gomez Award for contributions to the development of college baseball.

BILL "BOOTS" SIMONOVICH
February 8, 1933–July 20, 1973
Sunset Memorial Park, Minneapolis, Hennepin County (Metro Region); block 6, section 175, grave 4

The big center led Gilbert High School to the Minnesota High School basketball championship in 1951 and later was a star on the Minnesota Gophers. Simonovich died of a heart attack at the age of forty.

BRUCE SMITH
February 8, 1920–August 28, 1967
Fort Snelling National Cemetery, Minneapolis, Hennepin County (Metro Region); section O, grave 1474

After starring on the Faribault High School football team, Smith was a brilliant runner for *Bernie Bierman*'s national championship Minnesota Gophers in 1940 and 1941. Captain of the 1941 team, Smith also won the Heisman Trophy, given annually to the outstanding college football player in the nation. He is the only Gopher ever to win the award.

CAL STOLL
December 12, 1923–August 25, 2000
Fort Snelling National Cemetery, Minneapolis, Hennepin County (Metro Region); section 7, grave 107

Stoll played football for the Minnesota Gophers in 1949 and in 1972, two years after leading Wake Forest to an Atlantic Coast Conference title, returned to Minnesota as head football coach, the first former Gophers player to coach the team since *Bernie Bierman*. His 39–39 career record at Minnesota—which includes a bowl appearance and a 16–0 win over top-ranked Michigan in 1977— was unremarkable but still better than that of the coaches who followed. Stoll was the recipient of a heart transplant in 1987 and lived thirteen years after that, founding Second Chance for Life, a support group for heart transplant patients.

CLIFF THOMPSON
September 10, 1893–June 7, 1974
Eveleth Cemetery, Eveleth, St. Louis County (Northeast Region); block 6, lot 64, grave 1

Thompson coached the Eveleth High School hockey team from 1926 to 1958 and compiled a career record of 534 wins, 26 losses, and 9 ties. His teams won 78 straight games from 1948 to 1951 and four consecutive state championships. Thompson coached and helped to develop many stars at Eveleth, including Willard Ikola, Sam LoPresti, *John Mariucci,* and John Mayasich.

WES WESTRUM
November 28, 1922–May 28, 2002
Silver Creek Cemetery, Clearbrook, Clearwater
County (North Central/West Region)

A native of Clearbrook, Westrum entered professional baseball with the Crookston Pirates in 1940. He played briefly with the Minneapolis Millers before entering the military, where he was a paratrooper, and later played again with the Millers before being called up to the majors, with the New York Giants. Westrum played eleven seasons with the Giants. He became a coach when the Giants moved to San Francisco, but returned to New York in the 1960s and succeeded Casey Stengel as manager of the New York Mets in 1965. Westrum later managed the San Francisco Giants and then worked as a scout for many years for the Atlanta Braves.

ED WIDSETH
January 5, 1910–December 3, 1998
Sunset Memorial Park, Minneapolis, Hennepin County
(Metro Region); block 3, section 401, space 4

Widseth was a lineman on the Minnesota Gophers championship football teams under *Bernie Bierman* in 1934, 1935, and 1936. A two-time All-America, Widseth set up the tying touchdown in the Gophers' 1934 game at Pittsburgh, knocking the ball loose from a Pitt receiver on a punt. Minnesota later scored again to get its biggest win of the season en route to its first national championship. Widseth, who also played five seasons for the New York Giants in the National Football League, was inducted into the College Football Hall of Fame in 1954.

HENRY L. WILLIAMS
July 26, 1869–June 14, 1931
Lakewood Cemetery, Minneapolis, Hennepin County
(Metro Region); section 5, lot 251, grave 1

Williams served simultaneously as a football coach and physician at the University of Minnesota. One of the leading football strategists in the early-twentieth century, Williams devised a revolutionary offensive shift. He was the first full-time coach of the Gophers and led the team to a record of 136 wins, 33 losses, and 11 ties in 22 seasons. Williams was inducted into the College Football Hall of Fame in 1951. Williams Arena, home to the Gophers basketball team, is named after him.

FATAL ENCOUNTERS

CRIMES, DISASTERS, AND VICTIMS

At least when they are separated from us by time, criminals and victims can be viewed in a detached way, although often individuals become legendary even in their own era, as did the members of the James-Younger gang, whose murderous Northfield bank raid killed Joseph Heywood and Nicolaus Gustafson (*see* page 18).

Not all the victims suffered as the result of criminal activity. Those who did are sometimes diminished by the notoriety of their tormentors. Sunny Worel, a relation of murder victim Hedvig "Sammy" Samuelson, once said, "The fundamental problem remains. Who was Sammy Samuelson? In a way, she is sort of reduced as the victim. It's too bad, but her personality and who she was got lost to history."

ARMISTICE DAY BLIZZARD VICTIMS

Carl Iverson, June 24, 1898–November 12, 1940
West Lake Johanna Cemetery, Gilchrist Township,
Pope County (North Central/West Region)

Bror Kronborg, January 2, 1905–November 12, 1940
Forest Lawn Memorial Park, Maplewood, Ramsey County
(Metro Region); block 31, grave 205 A

Kermit Nordquist, March 6, 1912–November 12, 1940
Union Cemetery, Maplewood, Ramsey County
(Metro Region); block 2, lot 10

Melville Roberts, October 6, 1898–November 12, 1940
Acacia Park Cemetery, Mendota Heights, Dakota County
(Metro Region); Cypress section, block 9, lot 9, grave 9

M. Edgar Youngquist,
December 21, 1893–November 12, 1940
Forest Lawn Memorial Park, Maplewood, Ramsey County
(Metro Region); block 17, plat 2, lot 79, grave 4

The Armistice Day Blizzard of 1940 caught people by surprise across a large part of the country, including most of Minnesota. A storm system that had hit the West Coast a few days earlier reached Minnesota on November 11 (then called Armistice Day in honor of the last day of World War I and now celebrated as Veterans Day).

That fateful day, temperatures dropped, rain turned to snow, and gusting winds blew snow around. People found whatever shelter they could, but some did not survive. The death toll from the storm was listed as forty-nine in Minnesota. Many of the dead were duck hunters, including these five men from three hunting parties, all of whom froze to death on Prairie Island in Welch Township near Red Wing in Goodhue County. The date of death on each man's death certificate is given as November 12, because the men's bodies were found on that day.

BAUDETTE FIRE VICTIMS
Died October 7, 1910
Elm Park Cemetery, Baudette, Minnesota, Lake of the Woods County (North Central/West Region)

Forest fires broke out in northern Minnesota in the early fall of 1910. A fire that first ravaged Williams and Cedar Spur reached Baudette on October 7. Forty-two people in ten townships died in the conflagration. Twenty-seven of them are buried in unmarked graves in Elm Park Cemetery; thirteen of the victims remain unidentified.

ANN BILANSKY
1820–March 23, 1860
Calvary Cemetery, St. Paul, Ramsey County (Metro Region); section 1, unmarked grave

On March 13, 1859, two days after her husband, Stanislaus, died in St. Paul following a brief illness, Ann

Bilansky was arrested on suspicion of murder, along with John Walker, her nephew. Walker avoided a grand-jury indictment, but Bilansky was charged, and a sensational trial began in May.

The prosecution case was fueled by allegations of intimacy between Ann and Walker (with accusations that he was not really her nephew) and based largely on the testimony of a neighbor (herself accused by the defense of an affair with Walker) that Ann had purchased arsenic shortly before Stanislaus became ill. On June 3 the all-male jury of the time brought in a verdict of guilty. In late July Bilansky escaped from the Ramsey County jail but was captured a week later in Walker's company. Despite pleas for mercy and petitions alleging that she had not received a fair trial, Bilansky was sentenced to death. Governor *Alexander Ramsey* (whose brother, Justus, had been a jury member) refused to commute the sentence, and on March 23 Bilansky was hanged, the only woman ever to be executed in Minnesota. From the gallows she declared, "I will yet get justice in Heaven." Bilansky had become a Catholic the day before her death; she was buried in an unmarked grave in a Catholic cemetery.

CLAUS BLIXT & HARRY HAYWARD
Claus Blixt, June 9, 1853–August 21, 1925
Fairview Cemetery, Stillwater, Washington County (Metro Region); prison lot, line 4, number 67 (unmarked grave)

Harry Hayward, died December 11, 1895, at the age of 31
Minneapolis Pioneers and Soldiers Memorial Cemetery (Layman's Cemetery), Hennepin County (Metro Region); block D, lot 33

Blixt was the hired killer for Harry Hayward in the highly publicized murder of dressmaker "Kitty" Ging. A janitor at the Ozark Flats apartment building on Hennepin Avenue in Minneapolis—where he, Hayward, and Ging lived—Blixt shot Kitty while the two rode in a carriage in south Minneapolis on a December evening in 1894, then left her body near Lake Calhoun. Blixt received a life sentence, to be served at the Minnesota State Prison in Stillwater, where he eventually died.

Hayward was convicted of arranging the death of Ging (their exact relationship is unclear). Although he claimed to be innocent, Hayward later admitted to a news reporter his part in the murder, shortly before being hanged. His body was held in a vault at Lakewood Cemetery in Minneapolis before being dispatched to Chicago for cremation. The remains were then interred in the Hayward family plot in Layman's Cemetery. Reportedly, the body of Ging was sent to her hometown of Auburn, New York.

Claus Blixt, Harry Hayward, "Kitty" Ging, 1894

ISADORE BLUMENFELD ("KID CANN") & YIDDY BLOOM
Isadore Blumenfeld, September 8, 1900–June 21, 1981
Yiddy Bloom, January 28, 1911–November 18, 1994
**Adath-Yeshurun Cemetery, Edina, Hennepin County
(Metro Region); Blumenfeld: section 3, block 1, lot 9,
grave 2, Bloom: section 3, block 1, lot 10, grave 3**

Brothers Yiddy Bloom and Isadore Blumenfield (the spelling on his grave marker and death certificate, although the usual spelling is Blumenfeld and he was better known as "Kid Cann") are buried a few feet apart. They were well-known underworld figures although Blumenfeld gained far more notoriety, starting as a bootlegger during Prohibition. In the 1930s Blumenfeld was twice acquitted, once for the murder of crusading journalist Walter Liggett, who was investigating organized crime, and once for laundering ransom money obtained from the kidnapping of oilman Charles Urschel. Blumenfeld went on trial in 1960 for defrauding the former Twin City Rapid Transit Company. Although found not guilty on these charges, he was convicted in a separate trial for inducing a prostitute to cross state lines for immoral purposes. The following year, he was found guilty of attempting to bribe a juror. "You have led a bad life, Isadore," said Judge *Edward Devitt* as he sentenced Blumenfeld.

Along with Blumenfeld, who was in prison by this time, Bloom was convicted with two others of siphoning profits of nearly a million dollars from liquor stores and bars through a maze of syndicates, although the conviction was reversed on appeal. Some years later, Bloom was sentenced to a year in prison after pleading guilty to conspiring to manipulate a stock price.

Blumenfeld spent three-and-a-half years in prison in the 1960s, then moved to Miami where he and his brother, among others, invested in various properties. Examinations of real estate transactions by the *Miami Herald* in 1967 indicated that the brothers were associated with Meyer Lansky, a reputed Mafia member.

CHARLES COLLINS
Died March 7, 1902, aged 42
Minneapolis Pioneers and Soldiers Memorial Cemetery (Layman's Cemetery), Hennepin County (Metro Region); block 11, lot 16, 2nd grave (unmarked) from northeast corner

A cook at the San Angelo Hotel in Minneapolis, Collins was shot and killed by Herbert Gallehugh, whose wife worked as a dishwasher in the hotel kitchen. The shooting took place following a claim by Gallehugh's wife that Collins had propositioned her. Gallehugh claimed he went to the hotel merely to talk to Collins and was acting in self-defense when he shot him.

Gallehugh was found guilty of murder, and Susan Hunter Weir, Layman's Cemetery historian, credits the jury for convicting a white man charged in the death of a black man.

ELISABETH CONGDON
April 23, 1894–June 27, 1977
Forest Hill Cemetery, Duluth, St. Louis County (Northeast Region); section I, block 4, lot 2

Daughter of iron-mining magnate *Chester A. Congdon,* Elisabeth Congdon had inherited much of her father's fortune as well as the magnificent Glensheen mansion on Lake Superior in Duluth. Congdon had two daughters who stood to inherit her wealth. One of the daughters, Marjorie Caldwell, and her husband, Roger, were in need of money, and unsuccessfully sought to receive some from the trust that Congdon had set up for her daughters. On Monday, June 27, 1977, the morning nurse arrived at Glensheen and discovered the bludgeoned body of *Velma Pietila,* the night nurse, on the landing of the stairway. Inside her bedroom, Congdon had been smothered with a pillow.

Roger Caldwell was arrested and convicted of the murders. Marjorie Caldwell was acquitted of conspiring to murder in a separate trial, which featured new evidence that eventually led to the overturning of Roger Caldwell's conviction. The prosecutor and Roger then reached a plea agreement that allowed Roger to go free after more than five years in prison. The Caldwells divorced; Roger later committed suicide while Marjorie subsequently served time in Arizona for arson.

DULUTH LYNCHING VICTIMS
Elias Clayton, 1901–June 15, 1920
Elmer Jackson, 1898–June 15, 1920
Isaac McGhie, 1900–June 15, 1920

Park Hill Cemetery, Duluth, St. Louis County
(Northeast Region); section G, row 7, Clayton:
grave 15, Jackson: grave 14, McGhie: grave 13

A circus was in Duluth in the late spring of 1920 when
a seventeen-year-old white girl claimed that she had
been raped by six of the circus workers, all of them
black. Police made several arrests, and held the men in
the Duluth jail. That evening a mob stormed the jail
and were able to extricate three of the men—Elias
Clayton, Elmer Jackson, and Isaac McGhie. The rioters
held a "trial" for the men, then hanged them from a
light pole at the corner of First Street and Second Avenue
East. For many years, the three victims were buried in
unmarked graves at Park Hill Cemetery in Duluth. In
the 1990s, however, markers were installed, each with
the inscription "Deterred But Not Defeated." Only two
members of the lynch mob ever were tried and each
served less than half of a five-year sentence for rioting.
A memorial to the victims now stands near the site of
the lynching.

ALICE DUNN & FRANK DUNN
Alice Dunn, October 4, 1887–April 26, 1917
Calvary Cemetery, St. Paul, Ramsey County
(Metro Region); section 32, block 28, lot 1

Frank Dunn, October 23, 1873–February 26, 1958
St. Joseph's Cemetery, Rosemount, Dakota County
(Metro Region); on St. Patrick Dr. within cemetery

The 1917 killing of Alice Dunn spawned a number of
different murder trials, the most sensational being that
of her older husband, Frank, who was charged with
hiring a group of men to murder her. The Dunns were
estranged when three men, originally thought to be
burglars, broke into the home of Alice's parents, looked
for Alice, and then killed her. The shooter, Joseph Redenbaugh, also confessed to the kidnapping and murder of
Minneapolis policeman George Connery, who had

stopped Redenbaugh and an accomplice for speeding two days earlier. Frank Dunn was found guilty and spent the rest of his life in prison.

LINUS "SKEETS" EBNET
April 1, 1915–July 21, 1938
Seven Dolors Cemetery, Albany, Stearns County (North Central/West Region); section 3, row 2, lot 20

Playing for the Winnipeg Maroons of the Northern League, Ebnet was hit in the head by a pitch from Vince "Dutch" Clawson of Grand Forks in a game in Winnipeg on July 16, 1938, and died of injuries from the beaning five days later. Born and raised in Albany, Ebnet was in his fifth season in the Northern League, also having played for Grand Forks and Crookston before coming to the Maroons in 1937. In the off-season, he was attending St. John's University in Collegeville and was playing on the baseball team each spring before then joining his Northern League team for the summer. Skeets was a cousin of *Ambrose "Lefty" Ebnet,* a member of the Minnesota Amateur Baseball Hall of Fame.

FLOUR MILL EXPLOSION VICTIMS
Olie Shay, died May 2, 1878, aged 35
August Smith, died May 2, 1878, aged 33
Minneapolis Pioneers and Soldiers Memorial Cemetery (Layman's Cemetery), Hennepin County (Metro Region); Shay: block F, lot 75, grave 7 from north (unmarked), Smith: block K, lot 69, south half, unmarked grave

Shay and Smith are two of the eighteen victims who died in the explosion of the Washburn A Mill and five other flour mills in Minneapolis on May 2, 1878, a horrific industrial accident caused by the ignition of flour dust. A monument with the names of all eighteen men who were died in the explosion is in section 3 of Lakewood Cemetery.

WILLIAM HAMM JR.

September 4, 1893–August 20, 1970

**Oakland Cemetery, St. Paul, Ramsey County
(Metro Region); block 42, lot 8**

The grandson of *Theodore Hamm,* the company's founder,
Hamm served as chairman of the board of the Hamm
brewery. In 1933 Hamm was kidnapped in St. Paul by
members of the Barker-Karpis gang. He was released
unharmed after a ransom was paid.

HINCKLEY FIRE VICTIMS

Died September 1, 1894

**Lutheran Memorial Cemetery, Hinckley,
Pine County (Northeast Region)**

A mass grave contains the remains of 248 Hinckley residents who died in the horrendous fire of September 1,
1894, that ravaged Hinckley and much of the surrounding area.

LITTLE FALLS ACCIDENT VICTIMS

Alma Olson, August 6, 1893–August 1, 1953
Gustave Olson, July 10, 1878–August 1, 1953

**Crystal Lake Cemetery, Minneapolis, Hennepin County (Metro
Region); section S-15A, lot 348, Gustave: space 4, Alma: 5**

Clenora Starmack, June 10, 1913–August 1, 1953
Stanley Starmack, November 6, 1913–August 1, 1953

**Fort Snelling National Cemetery, Minneapolis, Hennepin County
(Metro Region); section C-14, Clenora: grave 10291, Stanley: 10292**

Ten people died on Saturday morning, August 1, 1953,
in a two-car accident on U.S. Highway 10 between
Little Falls and Camp Ripley, the second deadliest car
traffic accident in state history (*see Slayton accident
victims* for the deadliest).

The four people in one car were all Minneapolis
residents: Alma Olson; her husband, Gustuve; Alma's
daughter Clenora Starmack; and Clenora's husband,

Stanley. The six victims in the other car—all from Manitoba, Canada—were buried in Winnipeg.

MALL OF AMERICA MAN
Died February 19, 2003,
aged 25–35
Oakland Cemetery, St. Paul,
Ramsey County (Metro Region);
block 10, lot 35, unmarked grave

Forensic sketch of Mall of America Man, 2003

On the evening of February 18, 2003, a man was discovered lying on the ground outside the parking ramp of the Mall of America shopping center in Bloomington. He had either fallen or jumped from one of the ramp's upper levels. "Mall of America Man," as he was called by the staff of the Hennepin County Medical Examiner's Office, died the following morning, and his identity remained a mystery. He was to be buried on December 30, 2003, but interment was postponed as authorities pursued a lead that they hoped would help to identify him. When the lead did not pan out, burial was rescheduled. On January 13, 2004, Mall of America Man was buried at Oakland Cemetery as a U.S. Army chaplain from Fort Snelling presided over a graveside service before a small group of mourners who came because they felt that an unidentified victim especially deserved recognition. (*See also Joe Duffy, page 180.*)

MOOSE LAKE FIRE VICTIMS
Died October 12, 1918
Riverside Cemetery, Moose Lake,
Carlton County (Northeast Region)

A monument in Riverside Cemetery commemorates the forest fire that swept through Moose Lake on October 12, 1918, and marks the graves of a number of the fire's victims, including five members (Frank, Saima, Tyyne, Hjalmar, and Elma) of the Williams family.

Minnesota Home Guards and other rescue workers dug graves for Moose Lake Fire victims, watched by *Governor J. A. A. Burnquist* (hatless at center back), about October 14, 1918

GERALD "PEANUTS" PETERSON
December 12, 1925–July 24, 1948
**Oneota Cemetery, Duluth, St. Louis County
(Northeast Region); section D, block 6, lot 5, grave 1**

A speedy center fielder, Peterson was one of five members of the Duluth Dukes baseball team killed or fatally injured in a fiery crash on Minnesota Highway 36 in the village of Roseville while traveling from Eau Claire to St. Cloud in summer 1948. Peterson, along with teammates Don Schuckman and Gilbert Trible and manager George Treadwell, was killed instantly when a chemical truck crossed the center line and crashed into their bus between Western and Dale Streets. Another Dukes player, Steve Lazar, died at Ancker Hospital in St. Paul two days later. The driver of the truck, James Grealish, also died and is buried in Calvary Cemetery in St. Paul (section 80, block 40, lot 19, grave 4; Ramsey

County, Metro Region). Treadwell, who was driving the team bus, is buried in Calvary Cemetery in Superior, Wisconsin. Trible and Schuckman were buried in St. Louis, Missouri, and Lazar in Olyphant, Pennsylvania.

VIRGINIA PIPER
November 24, 1922–October 24, 1988
Lakewood Cemetery, Minneapolis, Hennepin County
(Metro Region); section 23, lot 11B, grave 15

A socialite and wife of retired investment banker Harry Piper, Virginia Piper was kidnapped from her home in Orono on July 27, 1972. After a one-million-dollar ransom was paid, she was found chained to a tree in Jay Cooke State Park. Two men were indicted just sixteen days before the statute of limitations expired. Both were convicted, but an appeals court overturned the convictions and the men were acquitted in a new trial. Some of the ransom money turned up in ensuing years but the entire cache has never been found.

MARY FRIDLEY PRICE
August 29, 1876–November 28, 1914
Lakewood Cemetery, Minneapolis, Hennepin County
(Metro Region); section 2, lot 521, grave 44

Mary Fridley was the daughter of a wealthy man, a descendent of the pioneer after whom the Minneapolis suburb of Fridley is named. She died on November 28, 1914, when she apparently fell from the river cliff near the Town and Country Club on East River Road. Her husband, Fred, stood to inherit some of her family wealth although he faced a few obstacles: he had never been divorced from his previous wife, meaning that Mary was not his legal wife. Also, more than a year after her death, Fred and an associate were charged with her murder. Fred was an ex-convict who had served time for assault with intent to kill. Mary, who had been buried in the family plot at Lakewood Cemetery, was

exhumed so an autopsy could be performed. In 1916
Fred was convicted of throwing her down the cliff,
along with her dog, and then smashing her head with
a large rock.

HEDVIG "SAMMY" SAMUELSON
November 17, 1903–October 16, 1931
**Crystal Lake Cemetery, Minneapolis, Hennepin County
(Metro Region); section N-A-15, lot 11, grave 11**

A North Dakota native with family in Minnesota,
Samuelson was living in Phoenix, Arizona, in 1931
when she and her roommate were allegedly murdered
by Winnie Ruth Judd, as the result of an argument between the roommates and Judd (although some believe
the women were killed by Jack Halloran, Judd's para-
mour). After shooting Samuelson and Agnes Anne Leroi,
Judd reportedly packed the bodies in a pair of trunks
and accompanied them on a train trip to Los Angeles.
The stench, along with blood leaking from the trunks,
led to the discovery of the bodies and the arrest of Judd,
who was found guilty of murder but avoided execution
when she was declared insane. The bizarre nature of
the case created enough publicity that the owner of the
duplex where the murders occurred sold tickets for
tours of the murder site.

SLAYTON ACCIDENT VICTIMS
Died April 21 & June 12, 1940
**Monument on Maple Rd. (old U.S. hwy. 59) in Slayton,
Murray County (Southern Region); accident site**

The deadliest two-car accident in U.S. history took place
early on the morning of Sunday, April 21, 1940, on U.S.
Highway 59 in Slayton. Twelve people were killed in
the accident that involved a car with six young people
from Murray County colliding with a car carrying seven
people, who ranged in age from eighteen to twenty-one
years old, from Jackson County.

From the Murray County car, Everett Johnson (born October 20, 1923) is buried in Slayton City Cemetery, Wayne Gamble (born September 5, 1925) in Highland Home Cemetery in Hadley, Ruth Fisher (born April 1, 1925) in Prairie Hill Cemetery in Fulda, and Irene Schwab (born June 12, 1922) in St. Gabriel Cemetery in Fulda. Brothers Harold and Lorens Tuynman are buried in Rock Valley, Iowa.

One member of the Jackson County car, Elmer Meyer, survived. Another, Cecil Jensen, died on June 12. The others were either killed instantly at the scene or died at the hospital a few hours later. Jensen (born January 23, 1919) and George Larson (born May 11, 1919) are buried in Riverside Cemetery in the city of Jackson, Leo Egge (born August 18, 1918) and Gordon Meyer (born February 4, 1919) in Good Shepherd Catholic Cemetery in Jackson, and Carl Falk (born February 7, 1920) in Hauges Cemetery in Belmont Township. Hollis Luff is buried in Unadilla, Nebraska.

Monument to Slayton accident victims, 2003

WISEL FAMILY
Died August 6, 1866
**Wisel Cemetery, Preble Township, south of Lanesboro,
Fillmore County (Southern Region)**

A solitary gravestone marks the graves of four members of the Wisel family, three of whom were among the sixteen victims of a flood on August 6, 1866, when water from the South Branch Creek roared down the deep and narrow valley, breaching mill dams and wiping out most of the Wisel family as they were having a gathering at their farmhouse. Only Jerusha Wisel (wife of David and mother of Ezra) survived as she was rescued, clinging to her mattress, several miles downstream of the house. Julia Wisel, aged 80, David Wisel, 56, and Jonathan Wisel, 12, died in the flood. Ezra Wisel, who died November 26, 1860, at the age of 22, is also buried here. After the flood, the creek was called Wisel Creek.

NOT AVAILABLE HERE

EX-MINNESOTANS ELSEWHERE

CREMATED

Some people who are cremated still have gravesites, but in many cases the ashes are given to the family or returned to the funeral home. The ashes may be spread in a place that was significant to the person, or they may remain in an urn atop a relative's mantel. It is also possible that they are interred at a later time. Those listed below were cremated without immediate interment. Often their final disposition is unknown.

BOB ALLISON (July 11, 1934–April 9, 1995), American League Rookie of the Year with the Washington Senators in 1959 and a member of the Twins, after the Senators moved to Minnesota, from 1961 to 1970.

PRIYANKA BHAKTA (February 2, 1995–August 25, 2003), outstanding child chess player who competed in the Minnesota State Chess Tournament while on a furlough from her hospitalization for leukemia, from which she died four-and-a-half months later.

ROSALIE BUTLER (July 10, 1922–August 3, 1979), controversial member of the St. Paul City Council in the 1970s who fought successfully to ban nude dancing in businesses that served liquor and to repeal the city's gay-rights ordinance.

GRATIA COUNTRYMAN (November 29, 1866–July 26, 1953), head of the Minneapolis Public Library from 1904 to 1936. The first woman director of a large public library system in the United States, she also served as president of the American Library Association.

CHARLES F. DIGHT (July 6, 1856–
June 20, 1938), doctor and Minneapolis alderman who lived
in a (now-vanished) tree house
near Minnehaha Creek, outside
of which hung a sign proclaiming "Truth shall triumph /
Justice shall be law." A propo-
nent of eugenics who had some
correspondence with Adolf
Hitler regarding this science

Charles F. Dight, about 1920

dealing with the social control of human mating and
reproduction, Dight also advocated the involuntary
sterilization of the unfit.

JOE DUFFY (June 1, 1920–October 5, 1990), civic leader
who headed the drive to sell bonds for the construction
of Metropolitan Stadium in Bloomington during the
1950s. Opened in 1956, the sports arena closed after
hosting its last game on December 20, 1981; later the
colossal Mall of America shopping center was built on
the site. *(See also Mall of America Man, page 173.)*

EVELYN FAIRBANKS (December 12, 1928–March 21,
2001), author of *The Days of Rondo,* a memoir of grow-
ing up in the African American Rondo neighborhood of
St. Paul, which later disappeared with the construction
of Interstate Highway 94.

WILBUR FOSHAY (December 12, 1881–September 1,
1957), developer of the tower bearing his name that for
more than forty years was the tallest building in Minneapolis. Foshay spent more than one hundred thousand dollars on a lavish, multi-day ceremony for the
opening of the Foshay Tower in August 1929. Within a
few months, however, he lost his fortune in the stock-
market crash. His financial problems led to legal misdeeds, and Foshay spent three years in a federal prison
for a variety of offenses, including mail fraud.

LAURENCE McKINLEY GOULD (August 22, 1896–June 21, 1995), explorer who served as Richard Byrd's second-in-command on Byrd's first trip to Antarctica and the president of Carleton College in Northfield, Minnesota, from 1945 to 1962.

NANCY HAUSER (November 20, 1909–January 17, 1990), choreographer, performer, and dance instructor.

LOYCE HOULTON (June 13, 1924–March 14, 1995), dancer and choreographer who studied with *Nancy Hauser* and later founded the Contemporary Dance Playhouse and School, which became the Minnesota Dance Theater and School.

SARAH "SALLY" ORDWAY IRVINE (December 23, 1910–November 1, 1987), philanthropist who donated money for St. Paul's Ordway Center for the Performing Arts.

NELLIE STONE JOHNSON (December 8, 1905–April 2, 2002), labor leader and civil rights activist and the first black person elected to citywide office in Minneapolis, serving on the library board when *Hubert H. Humphrey* was mayor in the 1940s.

BUZZ KAPLAN (March 30, 1924–June 26, 2002), member of the Minnesota Aviation Hall of Fame who died when his replica World War I plane crashed in a bean field west of the Owatonna airport.

COYA KNUTSON (August 22, 1912–October 10, 1996), first woman to be elected to Congress from Minnesota, representing the northwestern

Coya Knutson and her hotel owner-husband,
Andrew Knutson, in Oklee, 1954

part of the state, who lost her attempt for a third term in 1958, in part because of a campaign that included a plea from her husband to return to her family in his now famous "Coya Come Home" letter.

CHARLES AUGUST LINDBERGH (Charles A. Lindbergh Sr.; January 20, 1859–May 24, 1924), member of Congress from Minnesota and unsuccessful candidate for governor and the U.S. Senate. Lindbergh was cremated four days after his death with plans for his ashes to be scattered over the family homestead near Melrose from a plane flown by his son, aviator *Charles A. Lindbergh Jr.* Lindbergh's urn was interred at Lakewood Cemetery in Minneapolis for more than eleven years, however, before being taken by his family.

DAVE MOORE (June 4, 1924–January 28, 1998), actor, baseball lover, and a pioneer in local television, serving as the news anchor and host of various shows at WCCO television for a half century. Moore was cremated with his ashes scattered, according to his widow, Shirley, "in the flower garden that he dearly loved" in the yard of his home.

Dave Moore, weather caster Bud Kraehling, sportscaster Rollie Johnson, *E. W. Ziebarth* (front row, left to right) and other WCCO staff members, about 1955

SIGURD F. OLSON (April 4, 1899–January 13, 1982), influential conservationist and the author of many books, including *The Singing Wilderness.*

JEANNETTE PICCARD (January 5, 1895–May 17, 1981), Episcopal priest who was one of the first group of women ordained in a controversial ceremony in July 1974, as well as the first woman to enter space, a feat achieved in an 11-mile balloon ascent in 1934.

VELMA PIETILA (April 26, 1911–June 27, 1977), nurse who was murdered, along with her employer *Elisabeth Congdon,* at the Glensheen mansion in Duluth.

RAY SCOTT (June 17, 1919–March 23, 1998), original member of the broadcast crew for the Minnesota Twins and a nationally renowned announcer for many sports, particularly football.

THORSTEIN VEBLEN (July 30, 1857–August 3, 1929), author and economist who became an associate professor at Stanford University. A Midwest native and graduate of Carleton College in Northfield, Minnesota, Veblen was cremated at Cypress Lawn Cemetery in Colma, California, the remains being sent to Palo Alto, California.

ZOILO VERSALLES (December 18, 1939–June 9, 1995), shortstop for the Minnesota Twins in the 1960s and the American League's Most Valuable Player in 1965, the year the Twins won their first pennant after moving to the state.

E. W. ZIEBARTH (October 4, 1915–February 27, 2001), a longtime faculty member at the University of Minnesota and a commentator on international affairs on WCCO radio in Minneapolis who received two Peabody Awards for distinguished achievement in broadcasting, one of which was for a story he did on his own open-heart surgery. *(See portrait on page 182.)*

IN ANOTHER PLACE

Not everyone who made a mark in Minnesota ended up here. Many prominent natives, citizens, and even short-time but significant residents are buried somewhere else.

DAVE BANCROFT (April 20, 1891–October 9, 1972), member of the Baseball Hall of Fame for his sixteen seasons as a shortstop in the National League. He also managed the Minneapolis Millers in 1933 and the St. Cloud Rox in 1947. Bancroft is buried in Greenwood Cemetery in Superior, Wisconsin. As of June 2004, this is the closest grave of a Baseball Hall of Famer to Minnesota. (The closest dead Baseball Hall of Famer to the Twin Cities is Burleigh Grimes in Clear Lake, Wisconsin.)

MARGARET CULKIN BANNING (March 18, 1891–January 4, 1982), author of novels and short stories while living in Duluth and also an early advocate of women's rights. She moved to Tryon, North Carolina, in 1972 and is buried in Polk Memorial Gardens in Columbus, North Carolina.

HARRY BLACKMUN (November 12, 1908–March 4, 1999) and **WARREN BURGER** (September 17, 1907–June 25, 1995), Minnesotans who served together on the United States Supreme Court, Burger as chief justice from 1969 to 1976. Blackmun was the chief author of *Roe v. Wade* in 1973, legalizing first-trimester abortions in the United States. They both rest in the Supreme Court section of Arlington National Cemetery in Arlington, Virginia.

NINA CLIFFORD (August 3, 1851–July 14, 1929), St. Paul's most famous madam who operated a brothel near the city hall that catered to the city's elite and was particularly prominent during St. Paul's gangster era in the 1920s. She is buried in Detroit, Michigan.

EARL CRAIG (March 25, 1939–January 1992), native of St. Louis and civil rights leader in Minneapolis who was a murder victim, his dead body discovered on January 14. He is buried in St. Peter's Cemetery in Hillsdale, Missouri.

ARTHUR G. DONAHUE (March 19, 1913–missing in action, September 11, 1942), native of St. Charles who joined the British Royal Air Force as a volunteer in 1940 before the United States entered World War II. Donahue fought in the Battle of Britain; transferred to the Far East, he was one of the last pilots to fly out of Singapore. After returning to England, he disappeared over the English Channel and was later officially presumed dead. Donahue shot down a total of five enemy aircraft and was awarded the Distinguished Flying Cross.

CASS GILBERT (November 24, 1859–May 17, 1934), famed architect who practiced in St. Paul with James Knox Taylor and designed the Minnesota State Capitol before designing the Woolworth Building in New York City and the United States Supreme Court Building in Washington, D.C. Gilbert is buried in Ridgefield, Connecticut.

CALVIN GRIFFITH (December 1, 1911–October 20, 1999), team owner who brought major-league baseball back to Minnesota when he moved his Washington Senators to the state in 1961 (a St. Paul team previously had a brief stint in the majors in 1884). Griffith is buried in Fort Lincoln Cemetery, Brentwood, Maryland, outside the mausoleum containing his uncle, Baseball Hall of Famer Clark Griffith, who raised Calvin and his sister, Thelma.

TYRONE GUTHRIE (July 2, 1900–May 15, 1971), founder and namesake of the Guthrie Theater, established in Minneapolis in 1963. While Guthrie's time in the state was brief, his legacy remains strong in Minnesota. One of the foremost theater directors of the twentieth century, Guthrie was knighted in 1961 and now lies in a churchyard at Aghabog church in Newbliss, County Monaghan, Ireland.

ELIZABETH KENNY (September 20,1880 [some sources say 1886]–November 30, 1952), nurse who while working in the Australian bush country developed treatments unlike those prescribed by doctors for dealing with infantile paralysis (polio). Called "Sister"as was customary for nurses in Australia and England, Kenny served as a British army nurse during World War I. She traveled to the United States in 1940 to spread her treatment ideas, which were not well received until she arrived in Minneapolis, where her Sister Kenny Institute was established in 1942. Kenny is buried in Nobby, Australia.

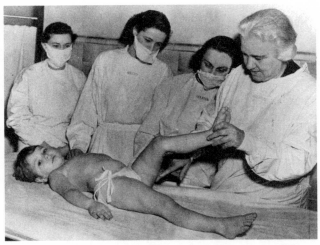

Sister Kenny demonstrated therapy techniques at her institute in Minneapolis, about 1942

CHARLES AUGUSTUS LINDBERGH (Charles A. Lindbergh Jr.; February 4, 1902–August 26, 1974), aviator who spent part of his childhood in Little Falls before making history in 1927 as the first person to fly solo and nonstop from New York to Paris. Lindbergh is buried in the

Kipahulu Hawaiian Churchyard along the Hana road on the Hawaiian island of Maui.

LITTLE CROW (Taoyateduta; about 1802–July 3, 1863), leader of the Kaposia band of Dakota and later a leader in the Dakota War of 1862. He is buried in Flandreau, South Dakota.

BILL MASTERTON (August 13, 1938–January 15, 1968), original member of the Minnesota North Stars in 1967 (after having played for two other Minnesota teams, Rochester and St. Paul, in the United States Hockey League) who scored the first goal in the North Stars' history. On January 13, 1968, Masterton suffered a head injury when he was checked and fell to the ice. He never regained consciousness and died thirty hours later, becoming the first player to die as a result of an on-ice injury in the history of the National Hockey League. Masterton is buried in Green Acres Memorial Gardens outside Winnipeg, Manitoba.

DOROTHY MOLTER (May 6, 1907–December 18, 1986), known as the "Root Beer Lady," for selling homemade root beer to canoeists who stopped by her cabin, and the last permanent resident of the Boundary Waters Canoe Area in northern Minnesota. She is buried in Union Cemetery in New Kensington, Pennsylvania.

ERNEST OBERHOLTZER (February 6, 1884–June 6, 1977), preservationist known for his work to protect the boundary waters of northern Minnesota and southern Ontario as well as the culture of the Ojibwe and other native people in the northern wilderness. Olberholtzer is buried in Oakdale Cemetery in Davenport, Iowa.

ROLLIN OLIN (August 17, 1839–March 8, 1910), lieutenant in command of the U.S. soldiers on September 23, 1862, at the Battle of Wood Lake, the decisive military struggle of the Dakota War, and later a judge advocate for the military commission appointed to try the Dakota who participated in the war. Olin, who was also prominent in early Minnesota baseball, is buried in Woodmere Cemetery in Detroit, Michigan.

MARIA SANFORD (December 19, 1836–April 21, 1920), first woman professor in the United States (at Swarthmore College in Pennsylvania in 1870) and the first woman professor at the University of Minnesota. Sanford served as professor of Rhetoric and Elocution from 1880 to 1909. A statute of Sanford represents Minnesota in the U.S. Capitol in Washington, D.C. She is buried in Mount Vernon Cemetery in Philadelphia.

CHARLES SCHULZ (November 26, 1922–February 12, 2000), creator of the *Peanuts* comic strip, grew up in St. Paul and began his artistic career with Charlie Brown, Snoopy, and his other beloved characters in the Twin Cities before moving to California. For his promotion of hockey in *Peanuts,* as well as for building a hockey arena near his California studio and then beginning a senior tournament at the arena, Schulz was inducted into the U.S. Hockey Hall of Fame in Eveleth, Minnesota, in 1993. He is buried in Pleasant Hills Cemetery in Sebastopol, California.

SANDY STEPHENS (September 21, 1940–June 7, 2000), quarterback on the 1960 and 1961 Minnesota Gophers football teams that went to the Rose Bowl. The first black ever to be named All-American quarterback, Stephens is buried in Restland Memorial Park in Monroeville, Pennsylvania.

TONI STONE (Marcenia Lyle Stone; July 17, 1921–November 2, 1996), athlete who grew up in St. Paul's Rondo neighborhood and played softball on city playgrounds. She switched to baseball after high school and later took the name Toni Stone because she "liked the

way it sounded." While visiting an ailing sister in San
Francisco in the 1940s, Stone ended up playing for the
San Francisco Sea Lions, a barnstorming semi-pro baseball team, as well as for the New Orleans Creoles. She
later played for the Indianapolis Clowns and Kansas
City Monarchs in the Negro American League. She was
the first woman in the Negro Leagues and was joined
by Mamie "Peanut" Johnson and Constance Morgan,
who played for Indianapolis. Stone continued living in
the Bay Area and died in Alameda, California. She is
buried in Golden Gate National Cemetery in San
Bruno, California.

Toni Stone in Creoles uniform, 1949–52

ROY WILKINS (August 30, 1901–September 8, 1981),
graduate of the University of Minnesota who became a
civil rights leader and head of the National Association
for the Advancement of Colored People in 1955. Wilkins
is buried in Pinelawn Memorial Park and Cemetery in
Farmingdale, New York.

North Central / West

Kittson
Roseau
Lake of the Woods
Lake of the Woods
Koochiching
Marshall
Pennington
Upper Red Lake
Red Lake
Lower Red Lake
Clearwater
Beltrami
Itasca
St. Louis
Polk
Norman
Mahnomen
Hubbard
Mississippi
Cass
River
Clay
Becker
Wadena
Aitkin
Wilkin
Otter Tail
Crow Wing
Mille Lacs Lake
Carlton
Todd
Morrison
Mille Lacs
Pine
Grant
Douglas
Kanabec
Traverse
Stevens
Pope
Steams
Benton
Big Stone
Swift
Kandiyohi
Meeker
Wright
Sherburne
Isanti
Chisago
Lac qui Parle
Chippewa
Anoka
Yellow Medicine
Renville
McLeod
Carver
Hennepin
Ramsey
Washington
Minnesota River
Sibley
Scott
Dakota
Lincoln
Lyon
Redwood
Nicollet
Le Sueur
Rice
Goodhue
Brown
Wabasha
Pipestone
Murray
Cottonwood
Watonwan
Blue Earth
Waseca
Steele
Dodge
Olmsted
Winona
Rock
Nobles
Jackson
Martin
Faribault
Freeborn
Mower
Fillmore
Houston

Red River
St. Croix River
Mississippi River

Northeast

Lake
Cook

Metro

Southern

CEMETERIES AND OTHER PLACES OF REST IN MINNESOTA

For the convenience of travelers, this appendix contains information about the cemeteries and other resting places in Minnesota that are mentioned in the guide. They are grouped into four major state regions: Metro (*see* page 193), Southern (197), Northeast (205), and North Central/West (208). See also the regions map on page 190.

Information for each cemetery includes the names of the individuals featured in this book who are buried there. Numbers in parentheses indicate the pages on which the main entries for the individuals can be found.

METRO REGION

CHISAGO COUNTY

NORTH BRANCH

Trinity Lutheran Church Cemetery. 12th St. & Cedar St.
Janet Johnson (87)

DAKOTA COUNTY

HAMPTON TOWNSHIP

Zion Cemetery. County hwy. 85, 1.2 miles
south of state hwy. 50.
Deil Gustafson (127)

HASTINGS

Lakeside Cemetery. 920 Nininger Rd.
Charles Powell Adams (43), Emma L. Brock (8)

MENDOTA HEIGHTS

Acacia Park Cemetery. 2151 Pilot Knob Rd.
Charles "Speed" Holman (19), Casey Jones (Roger Awsumb;
34), Harold LeVander (114), Melville Roberts (164),
Harold Stassen (111)

Resurrection Cemetery. 2101 Lexington Ave. S.
Anna Andahazy (29), Axel (Clellan Card; 29), John
Berryman (7), Edward Devitt (81), Guillermo Frias (127),
James J. Hill (128), Wally Karbo (150), Marty O'Neill (156),
John Roach (119), Larry Rosenthal (159), Bob Short (135),
Denis Wadley (27), Howard Wong (137)

ROSEMOUNT

St. Joseph's Cemetery. East side of state hwy. 3,
1 block north of 143rd St. W.
Frank Dunn (170)

HENNEPIN COUNTY

EDEN PRAIRIE

Pleasant Hill Cemetery. 12390 Pioneer Trail.
Jean Harris (85)

EDINA

Adath-Yeshuran Cemetery. 5605 France Ave. S.
Isadore Blumenfeld ("Kid Cann") & Yiddy Bloom (167),
Fanny Brin (79), Percy Ross (134)

MINNEAPOLIS

Crystal Lake Cemetery. 3816 Penn Ave.
Maceo Breedlove (140), Richard Green (25), Martin Layman
& Elizabeth Layman (69), Jim Mitchell (154), Alma Olson &
Gustave Olson (172), Hedvig "Sammy" Samuelson (176)

Fort Snelling National Cemetery. 7601 34th Ave. S.
Ferris Alexander (122), Tom Burnett (16), Albert Chesley (40),
Gleason Glover (17), Halsey Hall (32), Joe Hennessy (33),
Frederick M. Jones (130), Mary Kyle (35), Vernal "Babe" LeVoir
(152), C. Walton Lillehei (40), Ernest Lundeen (89), John
Mariucci (152), Bruce Smith (160), Clenora Starmack & Stanley
Starmack (172), Cal Stoll (161), Bruce Watson (136)

Hillside Memorium Cemetery. 2600 19th Ave. N.E.
Tony Jaros (149)

*Historic Fort Snelling. Five miles east of the Minneapolis-
St. Paul International Airport (take the Fort Snelling exits
on state hwys. 5 & 55).*
Whiskey (horse; 61)

Lakewood Cemetery. 3600 Hennepin County Ave. S.
Cedric Adams (28), Darragh Aldrich (Clara Aldrich; 7), Orion
Bartholomew (44), Bert Baston (139), James Ford Bell (124),
Anne Boardman (23), George Brackett & Millie Bronson (78),
LeRoy S. Buffington (8), J. A. A. Burnquist (108), Curt Carlson
(126), Stephen Chandler (47), Louis Cooke (142), Brian Coyle
(80), Borghild Dahl (24), Callum de Villier (30), William Dun-
woody (127), Adolph Eberhart (107), Mary Jackson Ellis (25),
Dick Enroth (31), flour mill explosion victims (171), William
Watts Folwell (25), Will Forshay (31), Orville Freeman (113),
Paul Giel (145), Bill Goldsworthy (146), Frances Cranmer Green-
man (9), Spencer Harris (148), Guy V. Howard (85), Hubert H.
Humphrey & Muriel Humphrey (86), Joe Hutton (149), Walter C.

James (Kim Wah; 129), Harry Wild Jones (10), Mike Kelley (151), Les Kouba (10), Carvel Lee (11), John Lind (106), Thomas Lowry (131), Franklin C. Mars (131), Bobby Marshall (153), Orianna McDaniel (42), Dorilus Morrison (90), Cecil Newman (35), Emil Oberhoffer (36), Floyd B. Olson (109), Rudy Perpich (115), John S. Pillsbury (104), Virginia Piper (175), Mary Fridley Price (175), Rocky Racette (158), Marion Savage (58), Thomas Schall (94), Dick Siebert (160), Lena O. Smith (95), Stew Thornley & Brenda Himrich (243), Tiny Tim (Herbert Khaury; 36), Selma Toy (37), Clara Ueland (97), Paul Wellstone (98), Reiko Weston (136), Henry L. Williams (163), Reuben Youngdahl (121)

Minneapolis Pioneers and Soldiers Memorial Cemetery (Layman's Cemetery). 2925 Cedar Ave. S.
Charles Christmas (64), Charles Collins (168), Harry Hayward (166), Martin Luther Nicks (51), Philander Prescott (74), Olie Shay & August Smith (171)

St. Mary's Cemetery. 4403 Chicago Ave.
Constance Currie (17), Elizabeth Quinlan (132), Louise Riordan (20)

Sunset Memorial Park. 2250 St. Anthony Blvd.
Bernie Bierman (139), Theodore Christianson (108), Lotus D. Coffman (23), Lew Drill (83), Julius Perlt (157), Bill "Boots" Simonovich (160), Rose Totino (136), Ed Widseth (162), Harriet Wolfgang (61)

Temple Israel Memorial Park. 4153 3rd Ave. S.
Jeanne Auerbacher (123), Albert Minda (119)

NEW HOPE

Gethsemane Cemetery. 8151 42nd Ave. N.
Curt Hennig (148)

RICHFIELD

Minneapolis Jewish Cemetery. 70 1/2 St. & Penn Ave.
Melvin Goldberg (84)

RAMSEY COUNTY

MAPLEWOOD

Forest Lawn Memorial Park. 1800 Edgerton St.
Bror Kronborg & M. Edgar Youngquist (164), Mao Vang Lee (20), Bruce Vento (97)

Union Cemetery. 2505 Minnehaha Ave. E.
Kermit Nordquist (164), Ron Ryan (21)

ROSEVILLE

Roselawn Cemetery. 803 Larpenteur Ave. W.
Alfred Brackett (46), Herb Brooks (141), Sarah Colvin (80),
Don (horse; 59)

ST. PAUL

Calvary Cemetery. 753 Front Ave.
Ann Bilanksy (165), Adolf Bremer (125), Pierce Butler (80),
Paul Henry "Lefty" Castner (142), Joseph Cretin (117),
Ignatius Donnelly (82), Alice Dunn (170), "Phantom" Mike
Gibbons & Tommy Gibbons (144), James Grealish (174),
Theodore Hamm (128), John Ireland (118), Emmanuel
Masqueray (12), Michael O'Dowd (155), Jacob Schmidt (134)

Elmhurst Cemetery. 1510 Dale St. N.
Alfred Gales (48), Tim Jones & Laser (police officer & dog; 21),
Tiger Jack Rosenbloom (133)

Oakland Cemetery. 927 Jackson St.
James Allen (44), Horace Austin (103), Harriet Bishop (22),
John W. Blair (15), Maud Borup (Maud Borup Kountze; 124),
Joseph Burger (46), Archibald Bush (125), Mary Colter (9),
Lyman Dayton (65), Ker Dunlop (143), Charles E. Flandrau
(84), Willis Gorman (100), Harlan P. Hall (33), William Hamm
Jr. (172), Herb Joesting (150), Lyman Kidder (49), Mall of
America Man (173), William R. Marshall (102), Andrew McGill
(104), Andrew I. Myrick (71), Arthur Nelson (91), Samuel
Phillips (51), Alexander Ramsey (99), Edmund Rice (93), Henry
Mower Rice (93), John B. Sanborn (52), Mary Schwandt
Schmidt (75), Marshall Sherman (53), Henry H. Sibley (101),
Pachao Xiong (56)

Science Museum of Minnesota. 120 W. Kellogg Blvd.
Don (gorilla; 59), Kuma (polar bear; 60)

WHITE BEAR TOWNSHIP

*St. Mary's of the Lake Cemetery. North side of
Stillwater St., .15 miles east of Otter Lake Rd.*
Francis X. "Moose" Goheen (146)

SCOTT COUNTY

BELLE PLAINE

Oakwood Cemetery. S. Buffalo St. & W. Park St.
Francis Bliss (45), John McConnell (50)

SAVAGE

Former site of Taj Mahal stables. Savage (across Minnesota River from Minnesota Masonic Home Bloomington, 11501 Masonic Home Dr., Bloomington).
Dan Patch (horse; 58)

WASHINGTON COUNTY

STILLWATER

Fairview Cemetery. 6373 Osgood Ave. N.
Claus Blixt (166), Samuel Bloomer (45)

SOUTHERN REGION

BLUE EARTH COUNTY

MANKATO

Glenwood Cemetery. 711 Glenwood Ave.
Maud Hart Lovelace (12)

BROWN COUNTY

NEW ULM

New Ulm Catholic Cemetery. Northwest quadrant of Cemetery Ave. & U.S. hwy. 14.
"Whoopee John" Wilfahrt (37)

St. Paul's Evangelical Lutheran Church Cemetery. West side of Cemetery Ave., 3/10 mile north of U.S. hwy. 14.
Don Dannheim (126)

SPRINGFIELD

City Cemetery. South side of county hwy. 24,
1/2 mile east of county hwy. 5.
Owen Haugland (18)

CHIPPEWA COUNTY

GRANITE FALLS

Granite Falls Cemetery. 135th St. SE, 6/10 mile
southwest of 30th Ave. S.E.
Andrew Volstead (98)

MONTEVIDEO

St. Joseph's Cemetery. South side of 60th St. SW, 7/10 mile
west of county hwy. 15 & 1/10 mile east of 12th St. S.W.
Antoine Joseph Campbell (63)

FARIBAULT COUNTY

WELLS

Rosehill Cemetery. North side of state
hwy. 109 at Half Moon Rd.
Dallas Hagen (148)

FILLMORE COUNTY

LANESBORO (SOUTH OF CITY)

Wisel Cemetery. Lerol Farm, south side of county hwy. 12,
1 mile west of bridge over south fork of Root River (on private
property).
Wisel family (178)

GOODHUE COUNTY

CANNON FALLS

Cannon Falls Cemetery. South side of
state hwy. 19 at 71st Ave. Way.
William Colvill (47)

FRONTENAC

Old Frontenac Cemetery. Green St.,
400 feet east of Van Blarcum St.
Arthur Ancker (39)

RED WING

Burnside Cemetery. South side of U.S. hwy. 61
at Cady St., 1 mile east of state hwy. 19.
A. P. Anderson (122), Eugenie Moore Anderson (78)

Oakwood Cemetery. East Ave. & 16th St.
Frances Densmore (9), Lucius Hubbard (104)

ZUMBROTA

Zumbrota Cemetery. County hwy. 6,
2/10 mile northwest of state hwy. 58.
Katherine Nye & Lillian Nye (42)

HOUSTON COUNTY

CALEDONIA

Caledonia Cemetery. W. South St. & S. Hokah St.
John Logan Willis (55)

Evergreen Cemetery. State hwys. 44/76 & West Main St.
Jedediah Pope (74), Hudson Wheaton (55)

JACKSON COUNTY

BELMONT TOWNSHIP

Hauges Cemetery. East side of U.S. hwy. 71,
1/10 mile south of county hwy. 28 (880th St.).
Carl Falk (177)

JACKSON

Good Shepherd Catholic Cemetery. East side of
U.S. hwy. 71, 1/2 mile south of county hwy. 34.
Leo Egge & Gordon Meyer (177)

Riverside Cemetery. East side of U.S. hwy. 71,
4/10 mile south of county hwy. 34.
Cecil Jensen & George Larson (177)

KANDIYOHI COUNTY

WILLMAR (NORTH OF CITY)

Vikor Lutheran Church Cemetery. West side of
county hwy. 5, 4.3 miles north of U.S. hwy. 12.
Guri Endresen-Rosseland (66)

LE SUEUR COUNTY

WATERVILLE

Sakatah Cemetery. Sakatah Cemetery Lane on south side
of state hwy. 60, 1/10 mile east of state hwy. 13.
Anna Dickie Olesen (92)

LINCOLN COUNTY

TYLER

Danebod Lutheran Cemetery. South side
of U.S. hwy. 14 at county hwy. 8.
H. Carl Andersen (77)

MCLEOD COUNTY

HUTCHINSON

Oakland Cemetery. Main St. S.
(state hwy. 15) & Oakland Ave. S.E.
Ancher Nelsen (91)

MEEKER COUNTY

DASSEL

Dassel Community Cemetery. East side of county
hwy. 4, 1/2 mile north of U.S. hwy. 12.
Paul Dille (48), Francis Johnson (130), Magnus Johnson (87)

LITCHFIELD

Ness Memorial Cemetery. 24040 580th Ave.
(1/2 mile north of county hwy. 23).
Acton settlers (62)

UNION GROVE TOWNSHIP

Burr Oak Cemetery. 343rd St., 2/10 mile north of
343rd St. at a point 1.6 mile west of state hwy. 4.
Fred Marshall (89)

MOWER COUNTY

AUSTIN

Calvary Cemetery. 1803 4th Dr. S.W.
Emil Scheid (159)

Oakwood Cemetery. 1800 N.W. 4th St.
George A. Hormel (129)

MURRAY COUNTY

FULDA

Prairie Hill Cemetery. Southwest corner of county
hwy. 39 (230th Ave.) & county hwy. 72 (31st St.).
Ruth Fisher (177)

St. Gabriel Cemetery. West side of county hwy. 40,
1/2 mile north of state hwy. 62.
Irene Schwab (177)

HADLEY

Highland Home Cemetery. North side of county hwy. 29
(105th Ave.), 1/10 mile east of county hwy. 86 (111th St.).
Wayne Gamble (177)

LAKE SHETEK STATE PARK

163 State Park Rd., Currie.
Lake Shetek settlers (69)

SLAYTON

Monument marking accident site on Maple Rd. (old U.S. hwy. 59).
Slayton accident victims (176)

Slayton City Cemetery. East side of U.S. hwy. 59, 7/10 mile north of state hwy. 30 (20th St.).
Everett Johnson (177)

NICOLLET COUNTY

FORT RIDGELY STATE PARK AND HISTORIC SITE

Fort Ridgely Cemetery. 72404 county hwy. 30.
Joseph LaFramboise (69), John S. Marsh (50), Hazen Mooers (71), Eliza Müller (71)

ST. PETER

Church of the Holy Communion. 118 N. Minnesota Ave.
William B. Dodd (66)

Greenhill Cemetery. Sunrise Dr. & Willow Dr.
George Engesser & Vates Engesser (31), John A. Johnson (107)

NOBLES COUNTY

WORTHINGTON

Worthington Cemetery. County hwy. 5 & Nobles St.
Stephen Miller (102)

OLMSTED COUNTY

ROCHESTER

Calvary Cemetery. 5th St. & 11th Ave. N.E.
Archibald "Moonlight" Graham (147)

Oakwood Cemetery. 41 7th Ave. N.
Merton Eastlick (66), Fred King (26), Charles Mayo & William Mayo (41)

REDWOOD COUNTY

MORTON AREA

*St. Cornelia's Episcopal Church. Reservation
hwys. 1 & 101, 2/10 mile off county hwy. 2.*
Andrew Good Thunder (Wakinyanwaste; 68), Samuel Hinman
(117); nearby: Mdewakanton Repatriation Burial Site: Marpiya
Oki Najin (Cut Nose; 70)

REDWOOD FALLS

Redwood Falls Cemetery. 759 N. Swain St.
Aubrey Dirlam (81), Thomas Wakeman (Wowinape; 76)

REDWOOD FALLS (NEAR CITY)

Lower Sioux Agency. 32469 county hwy. 2.
James Lynd (70), Andrew Robertson (27)

RENVILLE COUNTY

MORTON AREA

*Birch Coulee Battlefield State Historic Site.
County hwys. 18 & 2.*
Christian Marguth & Elise Marguth (49)

RICE COUNTY

FARIBAULT

Cathedral of Our Merciful Saviour. 515 2nd Ave. N.W.
Henry Whipple (120)

Maple Lawn Cemetery. 1917 4th St. N.W.
Francis Atherton Bean (123), Taopi (76)

NORTHFIELD

*Northfield Cemetery. East side of Division St.,
3/10 mile south of Woodley St.*
Joseph Heywood & Nicolaus Gustafson (18)

*Oaklawn Cemetery. North side of Wall
Street Rd. to east of Spring Creek Rd.*
Candace "Dacie" Moses (26), Karl F. Rolvaag (114), Ole E.
Rølvaag (13), Edward J. Thye (112)

ROCK COUNTY

LUVERNE

St. Catherine's Cemetery. West side of
U.S. hwy. 75, north of city limits.
Francis Sampson (51)

SIBLEY COUNTY

ARLINGTON

St. Mary's Catholic Cemetery. East side of
county hwy. 9, 2 miles north of state hwy. 5.
John McGovern (154)

WINTHROP

Winthrop Cemetery. West side of N. Brown St.,
2/10 mile south of state hwy. 19.
Mina Peterson (132)

WABASHA COUNTY

KELLOGG

Greenfield Cemetery (Cook's Valley Cemetery). North side
of county hwy. 18, 1.7 miles west of U.S. hwy. 61.
Levi Cook (65), Laura Linton (41)

WATONWAN COUNTY

ST. JAMES

Mount Hope Cemetery. West side of county
hwy. 27, 1/2 mile south of state hwy. 60.
Winfield Scott Hammond (107)

WINONA COUNTY

SARATOGA

Saratoga Cemetery. East side of state
hwy. 74, 4/10 mile south of county hwy. 10.
William Christie (47)

WINONA

St. Mary's Cemetery. Homer Rd. & county hwy. 105.
John Nett (155)

Woodlawn Cemetery. 506 W. Lake Blvd.
Rolla Banks (44), Charles E. "Charley" Goddard (48), William Mitchell (90), James A. Tawney (96), James Millard Tawney (53), Stephen Taylor (54)

YELLOW MEDICINE COUNTY

GRANITE FALLS (NEAR CITY)

Doncaster Cemetery. 255th Ave. (county hwy. 44) & Prairie's Edge Lane, 4/10 mile west of state hwy. 67.
Jerome Big Eagle (Wamindeetonka or Wamditanka; 63)

Upper Sioux Agency State Park. 5908 state hwy. 67.
Mazomani (70)

NORTHEAST REGION

CARLTON COUNTY

FOND DU LAC INDIAN RESERVATION (WEST OF CLOQUET)

Holy Family Cemeteries. East side of Ridge Rd. north of Reservation Rd.
William Cadreau ("Chief Chouneau"; 141), Joseph Naganub (Sits Ahead; 72), Lizzie Naganub (72)

MOOSE LAKE

Riverside Cemetery. East side of county hwy. 61, 1/10 mile north of state hwy. 27.
Moose Lake Fire victims (173)

COOK COUNTY

CHIPPEWA CITY (SITE OF FORMER OJIBWE [CHIPPEWA] SETTLEMENT, 1 MILE EAST OF GRAND MARAIS)

Chippewa Cemetery. Chippewa Cemetery Trail, 1/10 mile from state hwy. 61, near former Church of St. Francis Xavier.
George Morrison (13)

GRAND PORTAGE INDIAN RESERVATION

Holy Rosary Catholic Church Cemetery, Grand Portage. Upper Rd. (county hwy. 17) at Bay Rd.
Pete Gagnon (67)

ITASCA COUNTY

COLERAINE

Lakeview Cemetery. County hwy. 440 (Curley Ave.), 1 mile west of U.S. hwy. 169.
Lou Barle (138)

LEECH LAKE INDIAN RESERVATION

Inger Cemetery, Inger. Inger Rd. (Leech Lake Route 90) & Leech Lake Route 12.
Frank Rabbit (157)

KOOCHICHING COUNTY

INTERNATIONAL FALLS

St. Thomas Cemetery. Memorial Dr., 8/10 mile east of state hwy. 53.
Bronko Nagurski (154), Larry Ross (159)

LAKE COUNTY

BEAVER BAY

Chippewa Cemetery. Old Towne Rd., southwest of Lax Lake Rd. (county hwy. 4).
John Beargrease (15)

PINE COUNTY

ASKOV

Bethlehem Lutheran Cemetery. South side of state hwy. 23, 1/2 mile east of state hwy. 123.
Hjalmar Petersen (110)

HINCKLEY

Lutheran Memorial Cemetery. State hwy. 48 (Fire Monument Rd.), 1/10 mile east of county hwy. 140.
Hinckley Fire victims (172)

ST. LOUIS COUNTY

BOIS FORTE INDIAN RESERVATION

Nett Lake Cemetery, Nett Lake. Nett Lake Rd. at Lake Dr.
Charlotte Day (24)

CHISHOLM

Calvary Cemetery. 1/2 mile west of state hwy. 73 at northern city limits.
John Blatnik (78)

DULUTH

Forest Hill Cemetery. 2516 Woodland Ave.
George Barnum (123), Chester A. Congdon (126), Elisabeth Congdon (169), Paul Otis (156), Henry "Typhoid" Truelsen (96)

Grandma's Saloon & Grill. 522 Lake Ave. S., Canal Park.
Duluth Bear (59)

Lake Superior Zoo. 7210 Fremont St.
Mr. Magoo (mongoose; 60)

Oneota Cemetery. 6403 Highland St.
Leonidas Merritt (132), Willard Munger (91), Gerald "Peanuts" Peterson (174)

Park Hill Cemetery. 2500 Vermilion Rd.
Duluth lynching victims (Elias Clayton, Elmer Jackson, Isaac McGhie; 169), Olli Kinkkonen (20), Albert Woolson (55)

EVELETH

Eveleth Cemetery. Park Ave. & Hat Trick Ave.
Cliff Thompson (161)

HERMANTOWN

Sunrise Memorial Park. 4798 Miller Trunk Highway.
Wally Gilbert (145)

HIBBING

Hibbing Park Cemetery. Dillon Rd. &
U.S. hwy. 169/state hwy. 73.
Irene Bedard (30)

MEADOWLANDS

Meadowlands Cemetery. North side of
county hwy. 133, 1 mile east of Central Ave.
Maynard Speece (36)

VIRGINIA

Calvary Cemetery. State hwy. 135 & 9th Ave.
Frank Brimsek (140)

NORTH CENTRAL/WEST REGION

BECKER COUNTY

WHITE EARTH INDIAN RESERVATION

St. Columba Mission. 370th St.,
1/10 mile west of county hwy. 21.
Emily Peake (73)

BELTRAMI COUNTY

BEMIDJI

Greenwood Cemetery. 22nd & Bemidji Aves.
Charles W. Scrutchin (94)

Morell's Chippewa Trading Post. 301 Bemidji Ave. North.
Lobo (wolf; 60)

KELLIHER

*Paul Bunyan Memorial Park. East side of state hwy. 72
at Kelliher Rd., 2/10 mile south of Main St.*
Paul Bunyan (57)

BENTON COUNTY

SAUK RAPIDS

*Trinity Lutheran Church Cemetery. South side of 4th St.,
1/2 mile east of Summit Ave. S.*
Eldon John "Rip" Repulski (158)

CLAY COUNTY

MOORHEAD

*Prairie Home Cemetery. East side of 8th St.
between S. 7th Ave. & S. 10th Ave.*
Solomon Comstock (24), Wallace Douglas (83)

CLEARWATER COUNTY

CLEARBROOK

*Silver Creek Cemetery. South side of county
hwy. 49, 1/10 mile east of state hwy. 92.*
Wes Westrum (162)

CROW WING COUNTY

BRAINERD

Evergreen Cemetery. 1105 N.E. 3rd Ave.
C. Elmer Anderson (112), Roy Kuehmichel (130)

DOUGLAS COUNTY

ALEXANDRIA

Kinkead Cemetery. 530 Agnes Blvd. N.W.
Knute Nelson (105), Henrik Shipstead (95)

KITTSON COUNTY

KENNEDY

Red River Lutheran Church Cemetery. South side of 180th St., 1/4 mile east of county hwy. 1, Skane Township.
Odin Langen (88)

LAKE OF THE WOODS COUNTY

BAUDETTE

Elm Park Cemetery. North side of county hwy. 35 (7th St. S.W.), 1/2 mile east of county hwy. 1 (3rd Ave. S.W.).
Baudette Fire victims (165), Billy Noonan (36), Ted Rowell (134)

CLEMENTSON

Clementson Community Cemetery. East side of Koochiching County hwy. 18, 4/10 mile south of state hwy. 11.
Helic Clementson (64)

NORRIS TOWNSHIP

Wildwood Cemetery. South side of Winter Rd. Lake S.W., 1 1/2 miles west of Airport Forest Rd.
Mary Bender Cooley (143)

MILLE LACS COUNTY

PRINCETON

Oak Knoll Cemetery. 13th Ave. N. & W. Branch St.
Irvamae Applegate (22)

VINELAND

Vineland Cemetery. Western shore of Mille Lacs Lake on east side of unmarked road off U.S. hwy. 169, 1 mile south of Oodena Dr.
Arthur Gahbow (Wawenabe; 67), Batiste Sam (14)

OTTER TAIL COUNTY

FERGUS FALLS

Knollwood Memorial Gardens. West side of county hwy. 82,
1/10 mile south of Pebble Shores Dr.
Harry Burau (46)

Oak Grove Cemetery. E. Mount Faith Ave.,
1/10 mile south of Pebble Shores Dr.
Prince Honeycutt (149)

POLK COUNTY

CROOKSTON

Oakdale Cemetery. Memorial Dr., 1/2 mile west
of U.S. hwy. 2 (University Ave.).
Harold Hagen (84), Halvor Steenerson (96)

POPE COUNTY

GILCHRIST TOWNSHIP

West Lake Johanna Cemetery. West side of state hwy. 104,
2/10 mile north of county rd. 84 (312th St.).
Carl Iverson (164)

ROSEAU COUNTY

WARROAD

Indian Burial Grounds (formerly Highland Park Cemetery).
On former Ka-Back-A-Nung Trail, Carol St. N.W. & Jeans Dr.
N.W., 1/10 mile south of Lake St. N.W. (on private property).
John Ka-Ka-Gesick (118), Na-Ma-Pock (73)

STEARNS COUNTY

ALBANY

Seven Dolors Cemetery. Church Ave., 1/2 mile east of Eighth St.
Linus "Skeets" Ebnet (171)

AVON

St. Benedict Parish Cemetery. Chinook Ave.,
2/10 mile south of Sixth St.
George "Showboat" Fisher (144)

HOLDINGFORD

St. Mary's Cemetery. South side of county hwy. 17,
1/2 mile west of Riverside Rd.
Ambrose "Lefty" Ebnet (143)

ST. CLOUD

Assumption Cemetery. 2341 Roosevelt Rd.
Dick Putz (157)

North Star Cemetery. 1901 Cooper Ave. S.
Harold Knutson (88)

SAUK CENTRE

Greenwood Cemetery. Sinclair Lewis Ave. (county hwy. 17) &
county hwy. 185, 1 mile east of Original Main Street.
Sinclair Lewis (11)

SWIFT COUNTY

APPLETON

Appleton Cemetery. West side of state hwy. 119,
1/2 mile south of West Reuss Ave.
Elmer Benson (110)

NOTES

A selection of useful sources is included in the following notes. A key to the most-often used sources can be found in the bibliography following these pages.

All newspapers cited are Minnesota publications. Minnesota Historical Society (MHS), Minnesota Historical Society Press (MHSP), and Borealis Books (BB; an imprint of MHSP) items were published in St. Paul. University of Minnesota Press (UMP) items were published in Minneapolis.

INTRODUCTION
1. Information from Larry "Bucky" Bangs.
2. Tipton quote available at http://www.findagrave.com/rmn.html.

Acton settlers MHAH 121–22; **Adams, Cedric** MT Feb. 19, 1961, p. 1, 5; **Adams, Charles Powell** MHSC 4; **Aldrich, Darragh** WOM 334; **Alexander, Ferris** ST Mar. 1, 2003, p. A1, A20; **Allen, James** MOH; **Allison, Bob** BE 731–32, information from family; **Ancker, Arthur** DC, STPP May 16, 1923, p. 6; **Andahazy, Anna** DC, ST Dec. 3, 1983, p.1B, WOM 334; **Andersen, H. Carl** MT July 28, 1978, p.1B, 7B; **Anderson, A. P.** Anderson Center website at http://www.pressenter.com/~acis/history.html; **Anderson, C. Elmer** GM; **Anderson, Eugenie Moore** WOM 334, WAH, *Red Wing Republican Eagle,* Apr. 1, 1997, p. 1, 2; **Applegate, Irvamae** WOM 335; **Armistice Day Blizzard victims** DCs, *All Hell Broke Loose: The Story of How Young Minnesotans Coped with November 11, 1940, Armistice Day Storm* by William H. Hull (Edina, MN: W. Hull, 1985), x–xix, *Red Wing Daily Republican,* Nov. 11, p. 1, 2, Nov. 12, p. 1, Nov. 13, p. 1, 5, Nov. 14, p. 1–all 1940; **Auerbacher, Jeanne** WOM 335; **Austin, Horace** GM; **Axel** MT Apr. 14, 1966, p. 1, 9.

Bancroft, Dave BE 757; **Banks, Rolla** MCIW 1: 375, information from Dean Thilgen; **Banning, Margaret Culkin** MABP, *Duluth News-Tribune,* Jan. 7, 1982, p. 2A, WOM 336; **Barle, Lou** DC, *Grand Rapids Herald-Review,* Jan. 5, 1997, p. 1B, 2B; **Barnum, George** DC, City of Barnum website at www.ci.barnum.mn.us/; **Bartholomew, Orion** MT Sept. 18, 1919, p. 15; **Baston, Bert** TF 514, GS 30; **Baudette Fire victims** MHAH 270;

Cadreau, William DC, *Pine Knot* (Cloquet), Sept. 20, 1946, p. 7; Campbell, Antoine Joseph TDE 44, 46, 287–88, *The Commercial* (Montevideo), Jan. 17, 1913, p. 1; Cann, Kid *See* Blumenfeld, Isadore; Carlson, Curt MBP; Castner, Paul Henry SPPP Mar. 5, 1986, p. 1D; Chandler, Stephen MOH; Chesley, Albert MT Oct. 18, 1955, p. 13, Philip D. Jordan, *The People's Health: A History of Public Health in Minnesota to 1948* (MHS, 1953), 89, 176; Christianson, Theodore MS Dec. 10, 1948, p. 1, 22, GM; Christie, William *St. Charles Union*, Sept. 26, 1901, p. 1; Christmas, Charles Ruth Thompson, "C. W. Christmas: The Man Who Laid Out Our Streets," HCH 28 (spring 1969):12–13; Clayton, Elias *See* Duluth lynching victims; Clementson, Helic Baudette Region, Jan. 23, 1942, p. 1; Clifford, Nina Lance Belville, "Nina," *Minnesota Monthly* (Collegeville), Oct. 1981, p. 15–17; Clough, David MHSC 130, GM; Coffman, Lotus D. DC, James Gray, *The University of Minnesota* (UMP, 1951), 219, 263–374; Collins, Charles MT Mar. 8, 1902, p. 1, information from Susan Hunter Weir; Colter, Mary "News & Notes," MH 58 (winter 2003–04): 422, National Park Service website at http://www.cr.nps.gov/nr/feature/wom/2001/colter.htm; Colvill, William MHSC 134, MCW 13, FM; Colvin, Sarah WOM 343; Comstock, Solomon MHSC 135; Congdon, Chester A. DC, *Duluth Herald*, Nov. 21, 1916, p. 1, 10; Congdon, Elisabeth DC, City of Duluth website at www.ci.duluth.mn.us; Cook, Levi GMI; Cooke, Louis MT Aug. 20, 1943, p. 11; Cooley, Mary Bender DC, *Baudette Region*, July 28, 1930, p. 1; Countryman, Gratia WOM 173–89; Coyle, Brian DC, ST Aug. 24, 1991, p. 1A, 11A; Craig, Earl DC, Britt Robson, "Pride and Prejudice," *Mpls. St. Paul* (Minneapolis), Jan. 1990, p. 42–50, 130, 132, 134, 136; Cretin, Joseph MHSC 149–50; Currie, Constance WOM 343.

Dahl, Borghild WOM 344; Dan Patch MT July 12, 1916, p. 14; Dannheim, Don *Journal* (New Ulm), Aug. 23, 1999, p. 7A; Davis, Cushman MHSC 165, GM; Day, Charlotte ST May 6, 1989, p. 1B, 6B; Dayton, Lyman MHSC 169, LD website at www.daytonsbluff.org/LymanDayton.html; de Villier, Callum MT June 14, 1973, p. 15B; Densmore, Frances WOM 94–115; Devitt, Edward ST Mar. 3, 1992, p. 1A, 9A; Dight, Charles F. Gary Phelps, "The Eugenics Crusade of Charles Fremont Dight," MH 49 (fall 1984): 99–108; Dille, Paul *Dassel Dispatch*, Apr. 19, 1922, p. 1, information from Dassel Area Historical Society; Dirlam, Aubrey *Redwood Gazette*, June 5, 1995, p. 1, 5; Dodd, William B. DW 34, 36–38; Don (gorilla) Information from

Science Museum of Minnesota; **Don (horse)** SPPP July 27, 2003, p. 1B, 4B; **Donahue, Arthur G.** *Winona Daily News,* Sept. 9, 1990, p. 1E; **Donnelly, Ignatius** SPPP Jan. 2, 1901, p. 1, 2; **Douglas, Wallace** MBP; **Drill, Lew** SPPP July 6, 1969, p. 6, MT July 6, 1969, p. 14B; **Duffy, Joe** Charles Johnson, *Midwest Federal Presents History of the Metropolitan Stadium and Sports Center* (Minneapolis: Midwest Federal, 1970), 23–25, MT Apr. 1, 1955, p. 23; **Duluth Bear** *Duluth News Tribune,* Aug. 19, 1929, p. 1; **Duluth lynching victims** Michael Fedo, *The Lynchings in Duluth* (MHP, BB, 2000); **Dunlop, Ker** SPPP May 27, 1939, p. 1, 15; **Dunn, Alice, & Frank Dunn** DCs, MIM 201–18; **Dunwoody, William** DC, MT Feb. 9, 1914, p. 1.

Eastlick, Merton DW 23, *Rochester Post,* Nov. 13, 1875, p. 3; **Eberhart, Adolph** DC, MT Dec. 7, 1944, p. 7; **Ebnet, Ambrose** DC; **Ebnet, Linus** *Albany Enterprise,* July 21, 1938, p. 1, July 28, 1939, p. 1, MT July 22, 1938, p. 22; **Ellis, Mary Jackson** WOM 345; **Endresen-Rosseland, Guri** MHAH 105–7; **Engesser, George, & Vates Engesser** *St. Peter Herald,* May 24, 1962, p. 4; **Enroth, Dick** ST Mar. 24, 1999, p. C2.

Fairbanks, Evelyn *The Days of Rondo* (MHSP, 1990), SPPP Mar. 22, 2001, p. 1B, 6B, ST Mar. 22, 2001, p. B1, B9; **Fisher, George** ST May 18, 1994, p. 6B, BE 1016, GF correspondence with author; **Flandrau, Charles E.** MHSC 226, DW 34–39; **flour mill explosion victims** Shannon M. Pennefeather, ed., *Mill City: A Visual History of the Minneapolis Mill District* (MHSP, 2003), 100–103; **Folwell, William Watts** University of Minnesota website at http://www1.umn.edu/sesqui/history/features/folwell/feature06.html; **Forshay, Will** ST May 3, 2003, p. B8; **Foshay, Wilbur** Minnesota Public Radio website at http://news.mpr.org/features/200001/31_buzenbergb_foshay/index.shtml; **Freeman, Orville** ST Feb. 22, 2003, p. A1, A17, GM; **Frias, Guillermo** SPPP Feb. 22, 2004, p. 5C, ST Feb. 26, 2004, p. B1, B7.

Gagnon, Pete DC, *Cook County News-Herald* (Grand Marais), June 20, 1935, p. 1; **Gahbow, Arthur** DC, Mille Lacs Band of Ojibwe website at http://www.millelacsojibwe.org; **Gales, Alfred** Douglas E. Larson, "Private Alfred Gales: From Slavery to Freedom," MH 57 (summer 2001): 274–83; **Gibbons, Tommy, & Mike Gibbons** DCs, International Boxing Hall of Fame website at http://www.ibhof.com/ibhfhome.htm, SPPP Sept. 1, 1956, p.1, SPD Nov. 19, 1960, p. 1; **Giel, Paul** ST May 23, 2003, p. A1, A15; **Gilbert, Cass** Geoffrey Blodgett, *Cass Gilbert: The*

Early Years (MHSP, 2001); **Gilbert, Wally** *Duluth News Tribune,* Sept. 8, 1958, p. 8; **Glover, Gleason** DC, ST Aug. 25, 1994, p. 1A, 21A; **Goddard, Charles E.** MCW, 88–89; **Goheen, Francis X.** SPPP Nov. 14, 1979, p. 24; **Goldberg, Melvin** ST Sept. 1, 1998, p. B6; **Goldsworthy, Bill** ST Mar. 30, 1996, p. A1, A10; **Good Thunder, Andrew** *Morton Enterprise,* Feb. 29, 1901, p. 1, TDE 266; **Gorman, Willis** MHSC 267–77, GM; **Gould, Laurence McKinley** MBP; **Graham, Archibald** DC, *Free Press* (Chisholm), Aug. 26, 1965, p. 1; **Green, Richard** MBP; **Greenman, Frances Cranmer** MT May 25, 1981, p. 2B; **Griffith, Calvin** MBP; **Gustafson, Deil** ST Apr. 5, 1999, p. B5; **Gustafson, Nicolaus** *See* Heywood, Joseph; **Guthrie, Tyrone** MBP.

Hagen, Dallas *Wells Mirror,* Aug. 16, 2001, p. 5; **Hagen, Harold** *Crookston Daily Times,* Mar. 19, 1957, p. 1, 2; **Hall, Halsey** DC, **Hall, Harlan P.** MHSC 290—both, Stew Thornley, *Holy Cow! The Life and Times of Halsey Hall* (Minneapolis: Nodin Press, 1991); **Hamm, Theodore** MHSC 295, **Hamm, William, Jr.** DC, SPPP Aug. 21, 1970, p. 33—both, John T. Flanagan, *Theodore Hamm in Minnesota: His Family and Brewery* (St. Paul: Pogo Press, 1989); **Hammond, Winfield Scott** GM, MHSC 296, SPD Dec. 30, 1915, p, 1; **Harris, Jean** ST Dec. 15, 2001, p. A1, A16; **Harris, Spencer** Society for American Baseball Research, *Minor League Baseball Stars* (Cooperstown, NY: The Society, 1978), 20, 22, 52–53; **Haugland, Owen** DC, MT Aug. 4, 1929, p. 1, 2; **Hauser, Nancy** WOM 350; **Hayward, Harry** *See* Blixt, Claus; **Hennessy, Joe** ST Apr. 4, 2002, p. B9; **Hennig, Curt** ST Feb. 11, 2003, p. B1, B19; **Heywood, Joseph, & Gustafson, Nicolaus** George Huntington, *Robber and Hero: The Story of the Northfield Bank Raid* (MHSP, BB, 1986); **Hill, James J.** Martin Albro, *James J. Hill and the Opening of the Northwest* (MHSP, BB, 1991); **Hinckley Fire victims** MHAH 217–18; **Hinman, Samuel** DW 15, 79, 82; **Holman, Charles** Noel Allard, *Speed: The Biography of Charles W. Holman* (Chaska, MN: Allard, 1976); **Honeycutt, Prince** Information from Steven Hoffbeck, *Fergus Falls Tribune, Fergus Falls Weekly Journal*—both Jan. 31, 1924, p. 1; **Hormel, George A.** MBP; **Houlton, Loyce** WOM 351–52; **Howard, Guy V.** MT Aug. 22, 1954, p. 24; **Hubbard, Lucius** GM, MHSC 350; **Humphrey, Hubert H., & Muriel Humphrey** Carl Solberg, *Hubert Humphrey: A Biography* (1984; Borealis Books, 2003), BD; **Hutton, Joe** ST June 15, 1988, p. 10C.

Ireland, John Marvin R. O'Connell, *John Ireland and the American Catholic Church* (MHSP, 1988); **Irvine, Sally Ordway** DC, SPPP Dec. 5, 1982, p. 2D.

Walton ST July 7, 1999, p. A1, A13; **Lind, John** GM, MHSC 442; **Lindbergh, Charles A., Sr.** Bruce L. Larson, *Lindbergh of Minnesota: A Political Biography* (New York: Harcourt Brace Jovanovich, 1973); **Lindbergh, Charles A., Jr.** A. Scott Berg, *Lindbergh* (New York: Berkley Books, 1999); **Linton, Laura** DC, *Daily Post and Record* (Rochester), Apr. 3, 1915, p. 5; **Little Crow** Gary Clayton Anderson, *Little Crow: Spokesman for the Sioux* (MHSP, 1986); **Little Falls accident victims** DCs, MT Aug. 2, 1953, p. 1, 11; **Lobo** *The Story of Lobo* fact sheet from Morell's Trading Post, Bemidji; **Lovelace, Maud Hart** WOM 155–72; **Lowry, Thomas** DC, MHSC 452; **Lundeen, Ernest** MT Sept. 1, 1940, p. 1, 4, BD; **Lynd, James** MHSC 457, DW 12.

Mall of America Man ST Jan. 14, 2004, p. B1, B4; **Marguth, Christian, & Elise Marguth** DCs, Roy W. Meyer, *Everyone's Country Estate: A History of Minnesota's State Parks* (MHSP, 1991), 15–17; **Mariucci, John** TH 755; **Marpiya Oki Najn** (Cut Nose) MHAH 148–50; **Mars, Franklin C.** MBP; **Marsh, John S.** DW 16; **Marshall, Bobby** DC, GS 19, MT Nov. 11, 1906, First News sec., p. 1, 2; **Marshall, Fred** DC, ST June 7, 1985, p. 3B; **Marshall, William R.** GM, MHSC 490; **Masqueray, Emmanuel** DC, MHSC 493; **Masterton, Bill** MT Jan. 16, 1968, p. 19, 20; **Mayo, Charles, & William Mayo** Helen Clapesattle, *The Doctors Mayo* (UMP, 1941); **Mazomani** MHAH 184; **McConnell, John** BB 139–140, *Belle Plaine Herald,* June 3, 1943, p. 1; **McDaniel, Orianna** WOM 361; **McGhie, Isaac** *See* Duluth lynching victims; **McGill, Andrew** GM, MHSC 467; **McGovern, John** DC, GS 23; **Medary, Samuel** GM, MHSC 504; **Merriam, William** GM, MHSC 504; **Merritt, Leonidas** DC, *Duluth News Tribune,* May 10, 1926, p. 1, 2; **Miller, Stephen** GM, MHSC 511–12; **Minda, Albert** MT Jan. 16, 1977, p. 6A; **Mr. Magoo** *News-Tribune & Herald* (Duluth), Nov. 17, 1962, p. 1, Apr. 19, 1963, p. 1, 8; **Mitchell, Jim** Frank Bencriscutto et al., *Minnesota, Hats Off To Thee* (University of Minnesota Band Alumni Society, 1992), 106–7, ST Mar. 23, 2004, p. B2; **Mitchell, William** MHSC 515; **Molter, Dorothy** ST Dec. 19, 1986, p. 1A, 14A; **Mooers, Hazen** MHSC 519–20; **Moore, Dave** DM, *A Member of the Family: Letters and Reflections* (Minneapolis: Lazear Press, 1986), information from family; **Moose Lake Fire victims** MHAH 194; **Morrison, Dorilus** MHSC 526; **Morrison, George** *Cook County News Herald* (Grand Marais), Apr. 24, 2000, p. 1A, 2A; **Moses, Candace** DC, "A Free Hangout, But You Still Need Dough," *People,* June 9, 2003, p. 108, *Northfield News,* Jan. 8, 1981, p. 6; **Müller, Eliza** DW 26, 30; **Munger, Willard** ST July 12, 1999, p. A1, A6; **Myrick, Andrew I.** DW 6, 12, 14, 42.

Naganub, Joseph Mark Diedrich, *Ojibway Chiefs: Portraits of Anishinaabe Leadership* (Rochester, MN: Coyote Books, 1999), 107–14; **Naganub, Lizzie** *Duluth News Tribune,* Oct. 18, p. 1, 3, *Pine Knot* (Cloquet), Oct. 16, p. 1, *SPPP* Oct. 19, p. 1, 2—all 1931; **Nagurski, Bronko** GS 44, ST Jan. 9, 1990, p. 1A, 8A; **Na-Ma-Pock** *Warroad Pioneer,* Feb. 24, 1916, p. 1; **Nelsen, Ancher** ST Dec. 1, 1992, p. 1B, 4B; **Nelson, Arthur** SPPP Apr. 12, 1955, p. 1, 2; **Nelson, Knute** BD; **Nett, John** *Winona Daily News,* Jan. 26, 1999, p. 1A, 4A, 7A; **Newman, Cecil** DC, MT Feb. 8, 1976, p. 1A, 15A; **Nicks, Martin Luther** Information from Susan Hunter Weir; **Noonan, Billy** DC, *Baudette Region,* Feb. 20, 1957, p. 1; **Nye, Katherine, & Lillian Nye** WOM 365–66.

Oberhoffer, Emil HHC 50; **Oberholtzer, Ernest** Joe Paddock, *Keeper of the Wild: The Life of Ernest Oberholtzer* (MHSP, 2001); **O'Dowd, Michael** SPPP July 29, 1957, p. 1, 2; **Olesen, Anna Dickie** WOM, 226–46; **Olin, Rollin** Dean Thilgen, "General Henry H. Sibley's Connection to the Game of Baseball, 1985–68," available at http://halseyhall.org/history/sibleyandearlyminn baseball.pdf, Michigan death certificate information from DT; **Olson, Floyd B.** GM; **Olson, Sigurd F.** David Backes, *A Wilderness Within: The Life of Sigurd F. Olson* (UMP, 1997); **O'Neill, Marty** DC, SPPP Feb. 8, 1983, p. 1C; **Otis, Paul** ST Dec. 18, 1990, p. 4B.

Peake, Emily WOM 367; **Perlt, Julius** DC; **Perpich, Rudy** GM; **Petersen, Hjalmar** GM; **Peterson, Gerald** DC, *Duluth News Tribune,* July 25, 1948, p. 1, 8; **Peterson, Mina** DC, ST Mar. 6, 1996, p. B1; **Phillips, Samuel** MOH; **Piccard, Jeannette** WOM 367; **Pietila, Velma** DC; **Pillsbury, John S.** GM, MHSC 603; **Piper, Virginia** DC, ST Oct. 25, 1988, p. 1A, 12A; **Pope, Jedediah** *Caledonia Journal,* Mar. 3, 1909, p. 1; **Prescott, Philander** MHSC 615; **Preus, J. A. O.** GM, MHSC 615–16; **Price, Mary Fridley** DC, MIM 188–200; **Putz, Dick** DC, *St. Cloud Times,* Sept. 30, 1990, p. 3B.

Quinlan, Elizabeth WOM 368.

Rabbit, Frank DC, *Western Itasca Review* (Deer River), Nov. 10, 1994, p. 16; **Racette, Rocky** DC, *Minnesota Daily* (Minneapolis), Oct. 19, p. 1, MT Oct. 20, p. 1C, 4C—both 1981; **Ramsey, Alexander** GM, BD; **Repulski, Eldon John** *St. Cloud Times,* Feb. 11, 1993, p. 3C; **Rice, Edmund** BD; **Rice, Henry Mower** BD; **Riordan, Louise** WOM 368; **Roach, John** MBP; **Robertson,**

Andrew TDE 177; **Rolvaag, Karl F.** DC, ST Dec. 21, 1990, p.1A, 16A, information from family; **Rølvaag, Ole E.** DC, MBP; **Rosenbloom, Tiger Jack** SPPD Aug. 6, 2001, p. 1A, 5A; **Rosenthal, Larry** BE 1537, SPPP Mar. 5, 1992, p. 5C; **Ross, Larry** DC; **Ross, Percy** ST Nov. 14, 2001, p. B1, B9; **Roundhouse Rodney** *See* Jones, Casey; **Rowell, Ted** *Baudette Region,* Oct. 3, 1979, p.1; **Ryan, Ron, Tim Jones, & Laser** SPD Aug. 27, 1997, p. 1A.

Sam, Batiste *Mille Lacs County Times* (Milaca), Jan. 28, 1998, p. 12, WOM 370; **Sampson, Francis** Otto Friedrich, "Every Man Was a Hero," *Time,* May 28, 1984, p. 16; **Samuelson, Hedvig** SPPP Oct. 20, 1931, p. 1, information from family; **Sanborn, John B.** MHSC 667; **Sanford, Maria** WOM 77–93; **Savage, Marion** MBP; **Schall, Thomas** BD; **Scheid, Emil** DC, *Austin Daily Herald,* July 6, 1982, p. 1; **Schmidt, Jacob** SPD Sept. 3, 1910, p. 8; **Schmidt, Mary Schwandt** DC, MHSC 677; **Schulz, Charles** CS, *Peanuts: The Art of Charles M. Schulz* (New York: Pantheon Books, 2001); **Scott, Ray** DC, MBP; **Scrutchin, Charles W.** Steven R. Hoffbeck, "Victories Yet to Win: Charles W. Scrutchin, Bemidji's Black Activist Attorney," MH 55 (summer 1996): 59–75; **Shay, Olie, & August Smith** Information from Susan Hunter Weir; **Sherman, Marshall** MCW 25, FM; **Shipstead, Henrik** BD; **Short, Bob** DC, ST Nov. 21, 1982, p. 1A, 6A–7A; **Sibley, Henry H.** GM, Rhoda R. Gilman, *Henry Hastings Sibley: Divided Heart* (MHSP, 2004); **Siebert, Dick** DC, information from University of Minnesota sports information office; **Simonovich, Bill** DC, *Mesabi Daily News,* July 23, 1973, p. 2; **Slayton accident victims** DCs, MT Apr. 22, p. 1, 8, *Murray County Herald* (Slayton), Apr. 25, p. 1, 9, May 2, p. 1, June 20, p. 1, *Jackson County Pilot* (Jackson), Apr. 25, p. 1—all 1940; Gordon Meyer's name is spelled "Meyers" in newspaper accounts of the accident, on the death certificate for him, and on the monument—however, Gordon's last name and that of other family members on grave markers in Riverside Cemetery is spelled "Meyer"; **Smith, August** *See* Shay, Olie; **Smith, Bruce** GS 73; **Smith, Lena O.** DC, WOM 371–72; **Snana** MHSC 721–22; **Speece, Maynard** ST Sept. 29, 2001, p. B9; **Stassen, Harold** GM; **Steenerson, Halvor** *Crookston Daily Times,* Nov. 22, 1926, p. 1; **Stephens, Sandy** GS 96; **Stoll, Cal** ST Aug. 27, 2000, p. C1, C8; **Stone, Toni** WOM 333, *San Francisco Chronicle,* Nov. 6, 1996, p. B4; **Swift, Henry** BD.

Taopi MHSC 767, DW 61, 64, 65; **Tawney, James A.** MHSC 768, *Winona Weekly Leader,* June 20, 1919, p. 4; **Tawney,**

James Millard *Winona Independent,* Nov. 23, 1918, p. 6; **Taylor, Stephen** Kenneth Carley, "Revolutionary War Soldier Is Buried in Minnesota," MH 44 (summer 1975): 220–22; **Thompson, Cliff** DC; **Thye, Edward** GM, MBP; **Tiny Tim** ST Dec. 2, 1996, p. A1, A6; **Totino, Rose** DC, ST June 22, 1994, p. 1A, 16A; **Toy, Selma** DC, ST Aug. 22, 1986, p. 8B; **Truelsen, Henry** Ronald K. Huch, " 'Typhoid' Truelsen: Water and Politics in Duluth, 1896–1900," MH (spring 1981): 189–99, *Duluth News Tribune,* Dec. 11, 1931, p. 14.

Ueland, Clara WOM 374, Barbara Stuhler, *Gentle Warriors: Clara Ueland and the Minnesota Struggle for Woman Suffrage* (MHSP, 1995).

Van Sant, Samuel MHSC 807, GM; **Veblen, Thorstein** MHSC 809, MBP: **Vento, Bruce** BD; **Versalles, Zoilo** BE 1697–98; **Volstead, Andrew** DC, MBP.

Wadley, Denis ST May 5, 1994, p. 1B, 7B; **Wakeman, Thomas** MHAH 150, TDE 279–80; **Watson, Bruce** ST Mar. 20, 2004, p. B10; **Wellstone, Paul** BD; **Weston, Reiko** DC, Kathryn Koutsky & Linda Koutsky, *Minnesota Eats Out: An Illustrated History* (MHP, 2003), 47; **Westrum, Wes** BE 1728; **Wheaton, Hudson** *Caledonia Journal,* Apr. 15, 1896, p. 1; **Whipple, Henry** MHSC 846, DW 4, 71–72, 81–82; **Whiskey** SPPP June 15, 2002, p. 1B, 4B; **Widseth, Ed** GS 60; **Wilfahrt, "Whoopee John"** DC, *New Ulm Daily Journal,* June 16, 1961, p. 1, International Polka Hall of Fame website at http://www.internationalpolka.com/halloffame/1976/Wilfahrt.html; **Wilkins, Roy** MBP; **Williams, Henry L.** DC, MT June 15, 1931, p. 1, GS 8; **Willis, John Logan** UMB; **Wisel family** Wisel Cemetery information at www.rootsweb.com/~mnfillmo/cemetery/wisel.htm; **Wolfgang, Harriet** DC, ST June 13, 1980, p. 6B; **Wong, Howard** ST Sept. 21, 1993, p. 5B, MT Oct. 20, p. 1C, Oct. 26, p. 1D—both 1979; **Woolson, Albert** MCW xii, xiii, 195, MS Aug. 2, 1956, 1A, 10A.

Xiong, Pachao GMI.

Youngdahl, Luther GM, MBP; **Youngdahl, Reuben** MBP, MT Mar. 3, 1968, p. 1A, 14A.

Ziebarth, E. W. MBP.

BIBLIOGRAPHY

Each grave located in Minnesota has been visited by the author, who recorded the information on any grave marker found; sometimes this information does not agree with that given in other sources. The author has endeavored to include in this book what seems to be the most reliable information.

The sources listed below are the other items most often used by the author. In the following entries, MHS refers to the Minnesota Historical Society. For both the Minnesota Historical Society and the Minnesota Historical Society Press, the place of publication is St. Paul. Borealis Books is an imprint of the MHS Press.

Many of these sources can be consulted in person at the MHS Library in the Minnesota History Center. The Library's catalog is available on-line at http://www.mnhs.org/library/search/index.html. For further information, contact:

Reference Department
Minnesota Historical Society
Minnesota History Center
345 Kellogg Blvd. West
St. Paul, MN 55102-1906
E-mail: reference@mnhs.org
Fax: 651-297-7436
Telephone: 651-296-2143

Visit the MHS website at www.mnhs.org

BB *Brackett's Battalion: Minnesota Cavalry in the Civil War and Dakota War* by Kurt D. Bergemann. St. Paul: Borealis Books, 2004. **BD** Biographical Directory of the United States Congress website at http://bioguide.congress.gov. **BE** *The Baseball Encyclopedia: The Complete and Definitive Record of Major League Baseball* by Macmillan Publishing, 10th ed. New York: Hungry Minds, 1996.

DC Death certificate. MHS has the following microfilm copies of records maintained by the state Department of Health for deaths that occurred in Minnesota: death registers, 1899; death cards, 1900–1907; and death certificates, 1908–96. The certificates and cards from 1906 through 1996 are indexed through a searchable on-line database available at http://people.mnhs. org/dci/Search.cfm. (Check the on-line catalog for updates made as new resources are added to the MHS collections.) The microfilm may be searched in person at the MHS Library or borrowed through interlibrary loan. These services are explained in the Frequently Asked Questions (FAQs) that accompany the search site. **DW** *The Dakota War of 1862* (formerly *The Sioux Uprising of 1862*) by Kenneth Carley. 2nd ed. MHS Press, 1976.

FG Find A Grave website at http://www.findagrave.com. **FM** First Minnesota Volunteer Infantry Regiment re-enactors group website at http://www.firstminnesota.com.

GM Governors of Minnesota section of MHS website at www. mnhs.org. **GMI** Grave marker inscription (main source). **GS** *Gopher Sketchbook* by Al Papas. Minneapolis: Nodin Press, 1990.

HCH *Hennepin County History* journal, published by Hennepin County Historical Society, Minneapolis. **HHC** *Haven in the Heart of the City: The History of Lakewood Cemetery* by Mame Osteen. Minneapolis: Lakewood Cemetery, 1992.

MABP Minnesota Author Biographies Project at http://people. mnhs.org/authors. **MBP** Minnesota Biographies Project file, MHS Library, Minnesota History Center, St. Paul. **MCIW** *Minnesota in the Civil and Indian Wars, 1861–1865* by Minnesota Board of Commissioners on Publication of History of Minnesota in the Civil and Indian Wars. 2 vols. St. Paul, 1890–93. **MCW** *Minnesota in the Civil War: An Illustrated History* by Kenneth Carley. MHS Press, 2000. **MH** *Minnesota History* journal, published by MHS. **MHAH** *Minnesota History along the Highways*. Comp. Sarah P. Rubinstein. Rev. ed. MHS Press, 2003. **MHSC** *Minnesota Historical Society Collections*, vol. 14: "Minnesota Biographies, 1655–1912." Comp. Warren Upham & Rose Barteau Dunlap. MHS, 1912. **MIM** *Murder in Minnesota: A Collection of True Cases* by Walter N. Trenerry. MHS Press, 1962, 1985. **MJ** *Minneapolis Journal*. **MOH** Medal of Honor Citations section of U.S. Army Center of Military History website at http://www.army.mil/cmh/Moh1.htm. **MS** *Minneapolis Star*. **MT** *Minneapolis Tribune*.

PG Political Graveyard website at http://www.political graveyard.com.

SPD *St. Paul Dispatch.* **SPPP** *St. Paul Pioneer Press.* **SSDI** Social Security Death Index available at http://ssdi.genealogy. rootsweb.com/cgi-bin/ssdi.cgi. **ST** *Star Tribune* (Minneapolis).

TB *Total Basketball: The Ultimate Basketball Encyclopedia* by Ken Shouler et al. Toronto: Sport Classic Books, 2003. **TDE** *Through Dakota Eyes: Narrative Accounts of the Minnesota Indian War of 1862.* Comp. Gary Clayton Anderson & Alan R. Woolworth. MHS Press, 1988. **TF** *Total Football: The Official Encyclopedia of the National Football League.* New York: HarperCollins, 1997. **TH** *Total Hockey: The Official Encyclopedia of the National Hockey League.* Ed. Dan Diamond et al. Kansas City, MO: Andrews McMeel Publishing, 1998.

UMB Upper Mississippi Brigade website at http://umbrigade. tripod.com/articles/mn1812pioneers.html.

WAH Women in American History, Encyclopedia Britannica website at http://search.eb.com/women. **WOM** *Women of Minnesota: Selected Biographical Essays.* Ed. Barbara Stuhler & Gretchen Kreuter. Rev. ed. MHS Press, 1998.

INDEX

227

PICTURE CREDITS

The images in this book appear courtesy of the following persons and organizations. In some credits, the name of the photographer or artist, when known, appears in parentheses, along with any other additional information.

Chippewa County Historical Society—page 72

Hennepin County Medical Examiner's Office—page 173 (Ingrid M. Holley)

Minneapolis Public Library, Minneapolis Collection—page 129

Minnesota Historical Society collections, St. Paul—page ii, 8 (George W. Floyd), 12, 19 (Robert R. Blanch Photography), 22 (Andrew Falkenshield), 25 (David Brewster, © 2004 STAR TRIBUNE/Minneapolis-St. Paul; *Star Tribune* Newspaper Portrait Collection), 28 (George E. Luxton), 32 (Minneapolis *Star Tribune*), 34 *right,* 34 *below* (Eugene Powell), 38, 39 (Charles Alfred Zimmerman), 43 (Joel E. Whitney), 53 (Joel E. Whitney), 54, 58, 61 (Duane Braley; *Star Tribune* Newspaper Portrait Collection), 63 (Simon & Shepherd), 75 (Shepherd Photo Studio), 79 (Gene Garrett), 90 (E. L. Brand), 92 (Chambers), 94 *top* (Lee Brothers), 94 *bottom,* 101, 109 (Kenneth M. Wright Studios), 117, 118, 124, 135 (Terry Garvey), 139, 141, 145 (C. O. Erickson), 150, 151, 155, 159, 167, 174 (*St. Paul Dispatch*), 180 (Charles Fremont Dight Papers), 181, 182, 186, 189 (Ernest C. Withers)

Veda Ponikvar and The Doc Moonlight Graham Memorial Scholarship Fund—page 147

Star Tribune—page 133 (Rita Reed) © 2004 STAR TRIBUNE/Minneapolis-St. Paul

Stew Thornley, photographer—page 16, 21, 26, 30, 52, 56, 65, 87, 113, 177

University of Minnesota Intercollegiate Athletics—page 153

Marlene Wisuri, photographer—page 13

ABOUT THE AUTHOR

Stew Thornley is the author of more than thirty books, many of them dealing with Minnesota sports history, and has received a pair of national awards for base-ball research. He enjoys traveling, a hobby he combines with his love of cemeteries. Thornley has been to every grave of a member of the National Baseball Hall of Fame, a quest that has taken him across the United States as well as to Cuba, and more recently has crisscrossed the state in pursuit of the final resting places of notable Minnesotans.

BRENDA L. HIMRICH

Thornley lives with his wife, Brenda Himrich, in Roseville, Minnesota, although at some future date they will be together at Lakewood Cemetery in Minneapolis (section 34, row 3B, grave 3).

ALSO AVAILABLE FROM THE MINNESOTA HISTORICAL SOCIETY PRESS

**The Minnesota Book of Days:
An Almanac of State History**
by Tony Greiner

A fun and fascinating day-by-day account of Minnesota history, chronicling important events, famous firsts, notable individuals, and interesting incidents. A perfect gift for any fan of Minnesota history and trivia.

$13.95, paper, ISBN 0-87351-416-5

**Minnesota History along the Highways:
A Guide to Historic Markers and Sites**
Compiled by Sarah P. Rubinstein

A handy travel guide to more than 254 historic markers, 60 geologic markers, and 29 state historic monuments throughout the state.

$13.95, paper, ISBN 0-87351-456-4

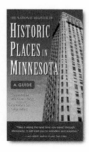

The National Register of Historic Places in Minnesota: A Guide
Compiled by Mary Ann Nord

A county-by-county guide to Minnesota's more than 1,500 holdings on the National Register of Historic Places, the country's official list of historic properties.

$13.95, paper, ISBN 0-87351-448-3

JOIN THE MINNESOTA HISTORICAL SOCIETY TODAY! IT'S THE BEST DEAL IN HISTORY!

The Minnesota Historical Society is the nation's premier state historical society. Founded in 1849, the Society collects, preserves, and tells the story of Minnesota's past through innovative museum exhibits, extensive collections and libraries, educational programs, historic sites, and book and magazine publishing. Membership support is vital to the Society's ability to serve its ever-broadening and increasingly diverse public with programs and services that are educational, engaging, and entertaining.

What are the benefits of membership?

Members enjoy:

- A subscription to the quarterly magazine *Minnesota History;*
- *Member News* newsletter and events calendar;
- Unlimited free admission to the Society's 25 historic sites;
- Discounts on purchases from the Minnesota Historical Society Press and on other purchases and services in our museum stores, library, Café Minnesota, and much more;
- Reciprocal benefits at more than 70 historical organizations and museums in over 40 states through Time Travelers; and
- Satisfaction of knowing your membership helps support the Society's programs.

Membership fees/categories:

- $65 Household (2 adults and children under 18 in same household)
- $45 Senior Household (age 65+ for 2 adults)
- $55 Individual (1 adult)
- $45 Senior Individual (age 65+ for 1 adult)
- $125 Associate
- $250 Contributing
- $500 Sustaining
- $1,000 North Star Circle

Join by phone or e-mail. To order by phone, call 651-296-0332 (TTY 651-282-6073) or e-mail membership@mnhs.org. Benefits extend one year from date of joining.

Six Feet Under was designed and set in type by Percolator, Minneapolis, who used Stone Serif, designed by Sumner Stone in 1987, for the text type. The book was printed by Transcontinental Printing, Peterborough, Ontario.